Where America's Black Leaders Learned to Lead

The Black College Career Guide

by Joan Carroll

A Zulema Publication ®

The information in **The Black College Career Guide** was compiled as a resource for students, parents, businesses, organizations and educational institutions. Efforts have been made to ensure accuracy of information, but errors may occur. In that event, we would appreciate your corrections and any other comments you may have regarding this publication.

The Black College Career Guide contains information made available by a number of sources. It is intended to be used as a reference guide only and more specific information should be obtained by contacting the school or scholarship source directly.

Where America's Black Leaders Learned To Lead
The Black College Career Guide
108 William Howard Taft Road
Cincinnati, Ohio 45219 USA

©Zulema Enterprises 1995

Cover Design by Hunter Graphics

Library of Congress Catalog No. 94-061536

ISBN 1-881223-05-01

Printed in the United States in America

To Pop, for being such an inspiration in my life.
To Mom, for teaching me "whatever you believe, you can achieve."
And to Skeeter, the only man who ever appreciated me as the
"wind beneath his wings."

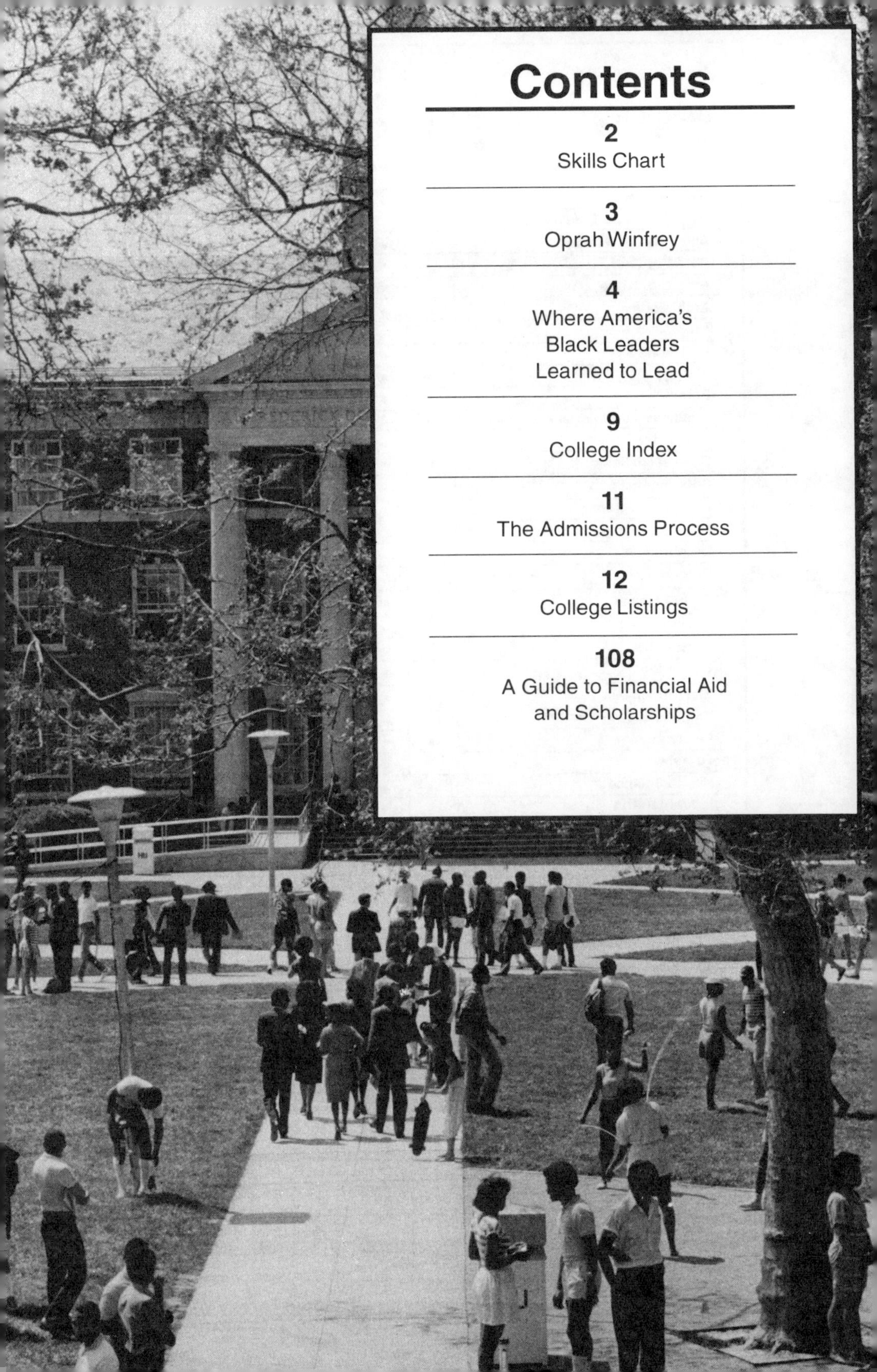

Contents

2
Skills Chart

3
Oprah Winfrey

4
Where America's
Black Leaders
Learned to Lead

9
College Index

11
The Admissions Process

12
College Listings

108
A Guide to Financial Aid
and Scholarships

CAREER CHOICE	Math	Science	English	Language	Art	Music	History	Performing Arts	Business
Accounting	•								
Agriculture		•							
Afro-American Studies			•	•					
Allied Health Fields	•	•							
Anatomy	•	•							
Animal Science		•							
Architecture	•	•							
Art					•				
Biochemistry	•	•							
Biology	•	•							
Botany	•	•							
Business Administration	•		•						•
Chemistry	•	•							
Clinical Medicine	•	•							
Communications			•	•					
Computer Science	•	•							
Criminal Justice			•						
Drafting	•	•			•				
Drama								•	
Earth Science	•	•							
Ecology		•							
Economics	•								
Education			•				•		
Electronics	•	•							
Engineering	•	•							
Finance	•	•							
Forestry		•							
Health Science	•	•							
Industrial Arts	•	•			•				
International Studies			•	•					
Journalism			•	•					
Law			•						•
Management	•		•						•
Marketing			•						
Mathematics	•	•							
Medical Sciences	•	•							
Medical Technology	•	•							
Microbiology	•	•							
Music Education			•			•			
Nursing	•	•							
Office Administration			•						•
Performing Arts								•	
Physics	•	•							
Pre-Medicine	•	•							
Psychology	•	•							
Secretarial Science			•						•
Urban Affairs		•	•						•
Veterinary Medicine	•	•							

"If you continue to further your education and strive to be your best, your boundaries are limitless!"

Oprah Winfrey
Tennessee State University

Oprah majored in Speech Communications and Performing Arts at Tennessee State University. In 1976, she moved to Baltimore to join WJZ-TV news as a co-anchor, and in 1978 revealed her talent for hosting talk shows when she became co-host of WJZ-TV's "People are Talking." Six years later, Oprah made the most significant move of her career. In January, 1984 she relocated to Chicago to host WLS-TV's morning talk show, "AM Chicago." In less than a year, the show was expanded to an hour and renamed **The Oprah Winfrey Show.** On September 8, 1986, the show was launched into national syndication by King World and immediately became the number one daytime talk show. Two years later in October, 1988, Oprah became the first woman in history to own and produce her own talk show. She and Harpo productions took over all responsibilities for **The Oprah Winfrey Show** from Capital Cities/ABC, Inc. Later that month, Oprah purchased a 100,000 square foot, state-of-the-art production facility in Chicago. The acquisition of Harpo Studios made Oprah Winfrey the third woman in history (behind Mary Pickford and Lucille Ball) and the first African-American to own such a facility.

Education is high on Oprah Winfrey's list of priorities, as demonstrated by her financial gifts to Tennessee State University, Morehouse College, United Negro College Fund, Desmond Tutu Educational Fund, the Harold Washington Library, the Corporate Community Schools of America, Chicago Academy of the Arts and a host of other institutions committed to excellence in education.

WHERE AMERICA'S BLACK LEADERS LEARNED TO LEAD

A quarter of a century after the civil rights movement, America's "historic and predominantly Black colleges" are still vital to the nation's higher education. Traditionally, these institutions have borne and still bear the brundt of responsibility for providing equitable educational opportunities for African-American students. The proof of their effectiveness is evident in the large number of Black College alumni who have succeeded against the odds. Some of the best and brightest minds in America were developed in the nation's historic and predominantly Black colleges and universities. While we can't name them all on these pages, here are a few of them.

Debbie Allen
Producer and director of NBC hit sitcom "A Different World."
Howard University

Lerone Bennett, Jr.
World-famous historical writer and journalist.
Morehouse College

Rev. L.V. Booth
Co-founder of the Progressive Baptist Convention, Inc.
Alcorn University

Ed Bradley
CBS News correspondent and co-editor of the Emmy Award winning "60 Minutes."
Cheney State College

The Calloways
Four-time Grammy nominees, Reggie and Cino are songwriters and record producers.
Kentucky State University

Spencer Christian
The nation's favorite weatherman can be seen weekdays on "Good Morning America."
Hampton University

Jylla Foster
She's the International Grand Basileus
of Zeta Phi Beta Dorty, Inc.
Livingstone College

Ossie Davis
Award-winning actor, director and
producer is also an accomplished
playwright.
Howard University

Terri Devard
A senior marketing manager for the
Pillsbury Company.
*Clark Atlanta University
School of Business*

Mayor David Dinkins
The first African-American to be
elected mayor of the City of New York.
Howard University

Joe Dudley
Successful entrepreneur is president
and CEO of Dudley products.
*North Carolina A&T
State University*

Marion Wright Edelman
President and founder of the Children's
Defense Fund.
Spelman College

Preston Edwards
Owns the publishing company
that produces *Black Collegiate
Magazine* and the *Journal of the NTA.*
Dillard University

Mary Hatwood Futrell
Only person to serve more than one
term as president of the National
Education Association (NEA);
currently is president of the World
Confederation of Organizations of
Teaching Professionals.
Virginia State University

Judge Deborah Gaines
This prominent female judge has
served on two Ohio courts.
*Central State University and
Howard University School of Law*

Judge Leslie Isiah Gaines
One of the nation's top African-
American criminal trial lawyers is
currently a judge.
*University of Maryland at
Eastern Shore and
Howard University School of Law*

Nikki Giovanni
The "Princess of Poetry," has won
numerous awards for her writings.
Fisk University

Earl Graves
The publisher of *Black Enterprise* magazine is well recognized for his business development skills.
Morgan State University

John Herring
As controller for Coor's Brewing Company, he oversees financial planning.
Grambling University.

Dr. Benjamin L. Hooks
The former executive director of the NAACP was the first African-American to head the Federal Communications Commission.
Lemoyne-Owen College and Howard University

Dr. John Henderson
This successful educator is the president of Wilberforce University.
Hampton University

Jesse Jackson
This human rights activist is the "Shadow Senator" for Washington, D.C.
North Carolina A&T State University

Mayor Maynard Jackson
Atlanta's popular mayor is currently serving his third term in office.
Morehouse College

Judith Jamison
The artistic director of the Alvin Ailey Dance Theater is known world-wide for her stage presence and dance style.
Fisk University

Arthur Johnson
IBM executive is president and chief operating officer of one of the firm's independent business units, IBM Federal Systems Company.
Morehouse College

Barbara Jordan
This famous former congresswoman recently served as a special assistant to the governor of Texas.
Texas Southern University

Spike Lee
Through his production company, *40 Acres and A Mule*, he has directed and produced award-winning films.
Morehouse College

George Lewis
Vice president and treasurer of Phillip Morris Company controls a $55 billion dollar budget.
Hampton University

Kathye Lewis
Former president of the National Technical Association (NTA) heads minority business development for Procter & Gamble.
Clark Atlanta University

Alfred Mays
This executive with Johnson & Johnson is president of two of the company's subsidiary divisions.
Hampton University

Patricia Russell McCloud
Prominent attorney is one of the nation's most popular professional orators.
Kentucky State University

Deborah McGriff
The first African-American female to serve as Detroit's general superintendent of schools.
Norfolk State University

Parren Mitchell
Former congressman from Maryland is chairman of the Minority Enterprise Legal Defense Fund.
Morgan State University

Thomas Revely III
Telecommunications executive is responsible for support services at Cincinnati Bell.
Central State University

Edwin (Ed) Rigaud
Vice president at Procter & Gamble has full technical, business and management responsibilities for a number of commercial products.
Xavier University at New Orleans

Joyce Roche
One of the highest ranking women in corporate America is in charge of global marketing at Avon.
Dillard University

Dr. Betty Shabazz
Widow of the Muslim leader, Malcolm X, she is a renowned educator and orator.
Tuskegee University

Joshua Smith
Entrepreneur is founder of MAXIMA Corp., one of the nation's largest minority-owned business; he also chaired the U.S. Commission on Minority Business Development.
Central State University

Dr. Louis Sullivan
First African-American to serve as U.S. Secretary of Health and Human Services.
Morehouse College

Art Thomas
This Central State graduate became the first alumnus to return and serve as the University's president.
Central State University

Barbara Van Blake
Director of human rights and community relations for the American Federation of Teachers.
Bethune-Cookman College

Alice Walker
She's the Pulitzer Prize winning author of "The Color Purple."
Spelman College

Gov. Douglas Wilder
The first African-American to be elected governor and head-of-state of the Commonwealth of Virginia.
Virginia Union University

Edward Williams
This regional marketing director keeps Upjohn Company competitive in the pharmaceutical industry.
Grambling State University

INDEX OF COLLEGES

12...ALABAMA A&M UNIVERSITY
13...ALABAMA STATE UNIVERSITY
14...ALBANY STATE COLLEGE
15...ALCORN STATE UNIVERSITY
16...ALLEN UNIVERSITY
17...ARKANSAS BAPTIST COLLEGE
18...ARKANSAS AT PINE BLUFF, UNIVERSITY OF
19...BARBER-SCOTIA COLLEGE
20...BENEDICT COLLEGE
21...BENNETT COLLEGE
22...BETHUNE-COOKMAN COLLEGE
23...BLUEFIELD STATE COLLEGE
24...BOWIE STATE COLLEGE
25...CENTRAL STATE COLLEGE
26...CHEYNEY STATE UNIVERSITY
27...CHICAGO STATE UNIVERSITY
28...CHAFLIN COLLEGE
29...CLARK ATLANTA UNIVERSITY
30...COPPIN STATE COLLEGE
31...DELAWARE STATE COLLEGE
32...DILLARD UNIVERSITY
33... DISTRICT OF COLUMBIA, UNIVERSITY OF
34...EDWARD WATERS COLLEGE
35...ELIZABETH CITY STATE COLLEGE
36...FAYETTEVILLE STATE UNIVERSITY
37...FISK UNIVERSITY
38...FLORIDA A&M UNIVERSITY
39...FLORIDA MEMORIAL COLLEGE
40...FORT VALLEY STATE COLLEGE
41...GRAMBLING STATE UNIVERSITY
42...HAMPTON UNIVERSITY
43...HARRIS-STOWE COLLEGE
44...HOUSTON-TILLOTSON COLLEGE
45...HOWARD UNIVERSITY
46...HOWARD UNIVERSITY COLLEGE OF MEDICINE
47...INTER-DENOMINATIONAL THEOLOGICAL CENTER
48...JACKSON STATE UNIVERSITY
49...JARVIS CHRISTIAN COLLEGE
50...JOHNSON C. SMITH UNIVERSITY
51...KENTUCKY STATE UNIVERSITY
52...KNOXVILLE COLLEGE
53...LANE COLLEGE
54...LANGSTON UNIVERSITY
55...LEMOYNE-OWEN COLLEGE
56...LINCOLN UNIVERSITY (MO)
57...LINCOLN UNIVERSITY (PA)
58...LIVINGSTONE E COLLEGE
59...UNIVERSITY OF MARYLAND AT EASTERN SHORE

INDEX OF COLLEGES

60...MEDGAR EVERS COLLEGE OF THE UNIVERSITY OF NEW YORK
61...MEHARRY MEDICAL COLLEGE
62.. MILES COLLEGE
63...MISSISSIPPI VALLEY STATE UNIVERSITY
64...MOREHOUSE COLLEGE
65...MORGAN STATE UNIVERSITY
66...MORRIS BROWN COLLEGE
67...MORRIS COLLEGE
68... NORFOLK STATE COLLEGE
69... NORTH CAROLINA A&T UNIVERSITY
70... NORTH CAROLINA CENTRAL UNIVERSITY
71... OAKWOOD COLLEGE
72... PAINE COLLEGE
73... PAUL QUINN COLLEGE
74... PHILANDER SMITH COLLEGE
75... PRAIRIE VIEW A&M UNIVERSITY
76... RUST COLLEGE
77... SAINT AUGUSTINE'S COLLEGE
78... SAINT PAUL'S COLLEGE
79... SAVANNAH STATE COLLEGE
80... SELMA UNIVERSITY
81... SHAW UNIVERSITY
82... SHORTER COLLEGE
83... SIMMON'S BIBLE COLLEGE
84... SOJOURNER-DOUGLAS COLLEGE
85... SOUTH CAROLINA STATE COLLEGE
86... SOUTHERN UNIVERSITY (BATON ROUGE)
87... SOUTHERN UNIVERSITY (NEW ORLEANS)
88... SOUTHERN UNIVERSITY (SHREVEPORT)
89... SOUTHWESTERN CHRISTIAN COLLEGE
90... SPELMAN COLLEGE
91... STILLMAN COLLEGE
92... TALLADEGA COLLEGE
93... TENNESSEE STATE UNIVERSITY
94... TEXAS COLLEGE
95... TEXAS SOUTHERN UNIVERSITY
96... TOUGALOO COLLEGE
97... TUSKEGEE UNIVERSITY
98... UNIVERSITY OF THE VIRGIN ISLANDS
99... VIRGINIA SEMINARY AND COLLEGE
100.. VIRGINIA STATE UNIVERSITY
101.. VIRGINIA UNION UNIVERSITY
102.. VORHEES COLLEGE
103.. WEST VIRGINIA STATE COLLEGE
104.. WILBERFORCE UNIVERSITY
105.. WILEY COLLEGE
106.. WINSTON-SALEM STATE UNIVERSITY
107.. XAVIER UNIVERSITY

THE ADMISSIONS PROCESS

Admissions requirements vary from institution to institution. However, there are some basic requirements which all schools will request. Very often students are threatened by the process of qualifying for admission to a college. Don't be discouraged by test scores and high school grades. Although these elements are an important part of the admissions process of most colleges and universities, they are not exclusive determinants in the admissions process. Other considerations such as recommendations, potential, character and attitude also factor into the acceptance decision.

Many schools recognize the fact that some minority students are openly discouraged from attending college. Students who are negatively influenced by peers, teachers and family can seriously doubt their ability to succeed academically. This is why more and more schools are making efforts to accommodate students with potential by providing conditional programs. Remedial courses help students overcome deficiencies and perform on the regular college course level.

Numerous types of tests are administered to high school students such as the SAT, ACT and CBAT. The purpose of these tests are to evaluate strengths and weaknesses. All colleges want their students to be successful and the admissions process is the first step in achieving this goal.

It is highly recommended to find out the admissions requirements of a variety of colleges and take courses that will satisfy these requirements. This does not mean that a complete college prep curriculum is needed. It simply means that specific courses can help prepare you for college work.

First Impressions Count. The recommended number of schools for a student to apply is between five and eight. Remember, no two schools are alike. One way to determine if you and a particular school are a good match is to use the information in this resource book. Each institution has its own history, costs, academic program, admissions requirements and personality.

Your application should include a well-written, self description or personal statement as well as a resume of your credentials, honors, involvements, skills, jobs, athletic talents, creative abilities or anything and everything else which says something about you and what you have done with yourself outside of the classroom situation. **DO NOT ASSUME** that anyone in any college admissions office is going to read between the lines. Keep in mind that your application represents you as a candidate. It is up to the individual school to decide whether they wish to accept you or not. Always allow time for thorough research, especially if an essay is required. Make certain you give each application a lot of thought.

Alabama A&M University
Normal, Alabama 35762
(205) 851-5000

History:

Alabama A&M University was founded in 1875 and today is a public, four year, coeducational university. The school is accredited by the Southern Association of Colleges and Secondary Schools.

Location and Enrollment:

The University is located on a 900-acre campus which is situated in the urban center of Huntsville. Sixty buildings comprise the institution's facilities. The current enrollment at the University is approximately 5,400.

Curriculum:

The University's academic calendar is based on the semester system. Degrees offered include Bachelors, Masters and Doctorates. Major and minor programs of study number more than 78, including Economics, Computer Science, Medical Technology, Physics, Biology, Health Science and Horticulture, Community Planning, Engineering Technology, Forest Operation, Teacher Education, Telecommunications, Agri-Business, Food Science and Fashion Design. Special programs offered are the 13 College Consortium and the Honors Program. The University also hosts the Army ROTC Program.

Financial:

Cost per semester for residents is $700; non-residents pay $1,550 room and board is $2,825 annually for non-residents. Approximately 74 percent of the total student body receive some amount of financial aid. Alabama A&M University offers the following aid programs: loans, grants, and employment. For further information contact the Director of Financial Aid of the University.

Alabama State University
Montgomery, Alabama 36195
(205) 293-4100

History:

Alabama State University is a public supported, coeducational Institution founded in 1874. Today, the school is accredited by the Southern Association of Colleges and Schools, the National Council for Accreditation of Teacher Education and the National Association of Schools of Music.

Location and Enrollment:

The University campus covers over 80 acres of land in the eastern section of the city Montgomery, Alabama.   The campus has 31 buildings with a library which houses over 250,000 volumes of literature. The estimated enrollment at the University is nearly 5,600 full-time students.

Curriculum:

The University specializes in comprehensive undergraduate and graduate training in Education (Early Childhood, Elementary, Secondary, Adult and Special Education). The academic calendar is based on the semester system with degrees offered in Bachelor of Arts, Bachelor of Science, Master of Arts, Master of Education, and Master of Science and Education Specialist. Undergraduate degrees are offered in disciplines such as Computer Science, Biology, Radio-Television-Film, Child Development, Political Science and Marine Biology. The University also offers Military Science in the Air Force ROTC.

Financial:

Tuition and fees at Alabama State University depend upon residency. Alabama State accommodates 90 percent of their students with some form of financial aid. The following are the programs in which the college participates: loans, grants, scholarships and campus-related employment.

Albany State College
Albany, Georgia 31705-2797
(912) 430-4600

History:

Founded in 1903, the College was established originally as the Albany Bible and Manual Training Institute and was supported by private and religious organizations. In order to meet the changing needs of society, the mission of the College has expanded over the years. In 1917, the Institution became a state-supported, two-year college, and in 1943 was granted a four-year status. Today, Albany State College is a progressive, growing regional college whose stimulating and challenging environment fosters personal development, social responsibility, cultural enrichment, innovative ideas and scholarly activities for co-educational students.

Location and Enrollment:

The 130-acre campus is situated in the urban center of Albany, which is located in Southwest Georgia. Approximately 3,500 students are enrolled.

Curriculum:

Albany State College has four schools: Arts and Sciences, Business, Education and Nursing and Allied Health Services. The College offers more than 35 major fields of study, including a transfer engineering program and a dual degree program with Georgia Tech. Several 2+2 programs with community colleges available as well as joint and early enrollment programs. Advance degrees are available in Accounting, Business Administration, Business Education, Management, Marketing, Economics, Finance, Criminal Justice, Nursing and Public Administration. Cooperative Education is also available.

Financial:

Out-of-state students can expect to pay approximately $7,242 per year living on-campus and $4,500 per year living off campus. For residents of the state of Georgia, the cost is approximately $4,500 for boarding students and $2,000 for non-boarding students. Albany State College provides financial assistance for eligible students, who, without such help, would be unable to attend.

Alcorn State University
Lorman, Mississippi 39096
(601) 877-6100

History:

Alcorn State University was established in 1871 on the site of Oakland College, a closed Presbyterian school for boys. The history-packed campus still has some of the original buildings of Oakland College, built in 1830, scattered among its modern structures. Alcorn State University has recently been designated as a bi-centennial campus.

Location and Enrollment:

Alcorn is located equal distances from Vicksburg to the North and Natchez to the South. The University is surrounded with the ruins of beautiful Windsor Castle and the gigantic Mississippi river several miles away. All of these historic sites lend support to the century-old buildings and moss-draped trees in a creative and historic setting. The current enrollment at Alcorn State is approximately 3,000.

Curriculum:

The academic structure of the University consists of six divisions: Arts and Sciences, Education and Psychology, Agriculture and Applied Sciences, Business and Economics, Nursing and Graduate Studies. The University offers the Bachelor of Science, Bachelor of Arts, Bachelor of Music Education and Master of Science in Education Degrees. Both day and evening classes are offered. Undergraduate majors and/or concentrations are offered in several areas. Graduate Degrees are authorized by the Board of Trustees, State Institutions of Higher Learning, and the State of Mississippi. Alcorn State University offers two degrees: The Master of Science in Education and the Master of Science in Agriculture. The Master of Science in Education Degree is designed to lead to AA Teacher Certification.

Financial:

The undergraduate student can expect to pay approximately $4,500 per year living on campus. All out-of-state students should add an additional $2,100 per year. Scholarships, work study, grants and loans are available to qualified students.

Allen University
Columbia, South Carolina 29204
(803) 254-4165

History:

Allen University was founded in 1870. The University is operated by the African Methodist Episcopal Church. Allen University is a four-year, coeducational Institution with a mission to educate its students to their fullest potential as well as academic and social growth.

Location and Enrollment:

The 20-acre campus of Allen University is located in the urban section of the city of Columbia, South Carolina. Eighteen buildings hold the Institution's knowledge along with the library which carries nearly 43,000 volumes. The student population at the University is approximately 350.

Curriculum:

The University's academic calendar is based on the semester system and the degrees offered include the Bachelor of Arts and the Bachelor of Science. Major programs include: Art, Biology, Business Administration, Business Education, Chemistry, Criminal Justice, Elementary Education, English, English Education, History, Middle Childhood Education, Music, Physical Education, Psychology, Secondary Education, Social Work, Sociology, Special Education, Gerontology and Secretarial Science.

Financial:

Current estimated cost at Allen University is approximately $6,600 annually for a student living on campus and $4,700 living off campus. Financial aid is available through the college to qualified applicants. There are approximately 95 percent of students at the University who meet these requirements. The following is a list of financial aid at the University: loans, scholarships, employment and grants.

Arkansas Baptist College
Little Rock, Arkansas 72202
(501) 374-7856

History:

Arkansas Baptist College, founded in 1884, is a four-year, coeducational, Liberal Arts Institution. The College is church-related with a primary purpose to provide an enriched curriculum with a Christian environment in order to promote well-balanced, healthy, accurate thinkers and effective Christian leaders.

Location and Enrollment:

The College is located in Little Rock, the state capital of Arkansas. Little Rock is known as the Twin City because of a river that separates north from south. Arkansas Baptist College is in North Little Rock. Three other colleges also exist in the Little Rock area. The current enrollment at the college consists of 400-600 students.

Curriculum:

Bachelor Degrees are offered in the following areas: Elementary and Secondary Education, Religion, Social Science, Sociology, Social Work, Business Administration, Computer Science and General Studies.

Financial:

Tuition varies upon credit hours. Average tuition is approximately $4,000 per year. Arkansas Baptist College participates in the following financial aid programs which are given to students based on need, as well as academic performance: Pell Grant, Supplemental Educational Opportunity Grant (SEOG), College-Work Study, and Guaranteed Student Loan (GSL). There is also a state scholarship which is made available to full-time students that meet the specific requirements established for various scholarships.

Arkansas at Pine Bluff , University of
Pine Bluff, Arkansas 71601
(501) 543-8000

History:

Formed and created by an act of the Arkansas Legislature in 1872, the University (formerly Arkansas A.M and N.), is a state-funded, land-grant institution. The University is currently the largest institution of higher learning in Southeast Arkansas. History notes that the University has a reputation for the outstanding success and contributions of its graduates in Education, Government and Medicine.

Location and Enrollment:

The University is located in Pine Bluff, Jefferson County, Arkansas. Situated near Martha Mitchell Highway, the urban city has a population of approximately 6,600. It's also near shopping malls and theaters. The current enrollment at the University is nearly 4,000.

Curriculum:

Baccalaureate Degrees are offered in Accounting, Agricultural Economics, Agricultural Education, Agronomy, Animal Science, Art Education, Automotive Technology/Management, Biology, Biology Education, Business Education, Chemistry, Chemistry Education, Child and Family Development, Computer Science, Economics, Elementary Education, English, Fashion Merchandising, Foods, Nutrition and Institutional Food Services, Functional Art, Gerontology, Health and Physical Education, History, Home Economics, Industrial Arts, Mathematics, Music, Nursing, Parks and Community Recreation, Physics, Political Science, Psychology, Social Science, Social Welfare, Sociology, Special Education, Speech and Drama, Trade and Industrial Education.

Financial:

Residents pay $732, non-Residents pay $1,690 for tuition per semester. Room and board on average is $1,500. The Institution participates in the Federal Grant Programs such as: Pell, Work Study, Supplemental Education Opportunity Grant, Various student and loan programs. Scholarships are also available

Barber-Scotia College
Concord, North Carolina 28025
(704) 786-5171

History:

Barber-Scotia College was founded in 1867 by Rev. Luke Dorland, and today is an accredited, four-year, independent, non-profit coeducational Institution affiliated with the Presbyterian Church. A complementary feature of the College is its design as a small Liberal Arts Institution whose mission is the total development of its students--intellectually, physically, emotionally, socially and spiritually.

Location and Enrollment:

Barber-Scotia's 40-acre campus is located in Concord, North Carolina, a city of approximately 27,000. It is served by Southern Railway and Greyhound Bus Lines. Major highways are U.S. 29, North Carolina 49 and I-85. Charlotte-Douglas International Airport is only 30 miles away. There are approximately 700 students enrolled at Barber-Scotia College. They come from fifteen or more states, the District of Columbia, the U.S. Virgin Islands, Africa and other countries. Although a large number of students come from the Carolinas, the broad based geographical distribution allows for cultural and regional variety.

Curriculum:

Barber-Scotia College offers degrees in the Bachelor of Arts and the Bachelor of Science. The College also offers courses in over 10 undergraduate fields of study including Hotel/Restaurant Management, Marketing, Pre-engineering, Pre-nursing and Medical Technology. Cooperative Education is also available. Barber-Scotia College is fully accredited by the Southern Association of Colleges and Schools and the North Carolina State Board of Education. The institution also holds membership in the United Negro College Fund.

Financial:

Current estimated cost at Barber-Scotia College is $7,300 annually for a student living on campus, and $4,100 living off campus. Financial aid to students is available.

Benedict College
Columbia, South Carolina 29204
(803) 256-4220

History:

Since its founding in 1870, Benedict College has been carrying out the purpose stated in its original charter: to help shape students into "a power for good in society." A private, coeducational, liberal arts college, Benedict has a continuing, supportive relationship with the Baptist Church. It is fully accredited by the Southern Association of Colleges and Schools and is a member of the United Negro College Fund.

Location and Enrollment:

The 20-acre campus is situated in the urban center of Columbia. Twenty-two buildings comprise the Institution's facilities. Residence halls have a total capacity of 1,200. Seventy-five percent of the student body lives on campus. The enrollment at the College exceeds 1,600.

Curriculum:

Benedict College's academic calendar is based on the semester system. The College offers the Bachelor's Degree in 22 areas under four academic divisions. Courses include Business Administration, Computer Science, Criminal Justice, History, Accounting, Religion/Theology and Early Childhood Education. Benedict also has an active ROTC Program.

Financial:

For in-state and out-of-state students, the cost for attending Benedict is $4,213 per semester for a student living on-campus and $2,767 living off-campus. More than 85 percent of Benedict's students receive financial aid awards. Types of financial aid available at the College include grants, loans, scholarships and awards, work study and work aid.

Bennett College
Greensboro, North Carolina 27401-3239
(919) 273-4431

History:

Bennett College was established in 1873 as a regular public school. It was chartered as a college by the state of North Carolina in March 1889, and became a college for women in 1926. The College has been accredited by the Southern Association of Colleges and Schools. The historically black college was developed out of a unique social need at the close of the Civil War. Bennett College has an outstanding heritage in helping the mainstream of American society.

Location and Enrollment:

Bennett College has an average enrollment of 600 students. Forty-six percent are from North Carolina while others are from six foreign countries and all over the United States.

Curriculum:

Degree programs offered at Bennett College include B.A., B.S., Bachelor of Fine Arts and Bachelor of Arts and Science in Interdisciplinary Studies. Various majors include Education, Humanities, Social Science, and Sciences. The College offers concentration in a single field of study, in a combination of studies across departmental or division lines, or design of a special program of study in Interdisciplinary Studies. First year students take Communications, Mathematics, Science, Social Science and Physical Education. All students enroll in the Comprehensive Communications Skills Program.

Financial:

Annual tuition and fees for an average student are approximately $5,400(off-campus) and $8,920(on-campus). North Carolina residents can deduct $1,100 for the North Carolina Legislative Tuition Grant. There are many sources of financial aid-state and federal programs, as well as private sources that can ease the financial burden of paying for a college education. The Financial Aid Office recommends that all applying and returning students submit college and federal applications for financial assistance. Aid is offered in the form of academic scholarships, Pell Grants, loans, and campus work study.

Bethune-Cookman College
Daytona Beach, Florida 32114-3099
(904) 255-1401

History:

Bethune-Cookman College is a United Methodist Church-related, liberal arts, career oriented, coeducational and residential college founded in 1904 by one of America's most outstanding citizens, Dr. Mary McLeod Bethune. The College serves the needs of its students in education by providing a wide variety of learning experiences and programs designed to enable the students to become leaders with a sense of self-fulfillment and service to fellow human beings.

Location and Enrollment:

The College is located in an urban section of Daytona Beach, Florida. The 52-acre main campus contains 31 buildings and a library with over 193,000 books and audio visual materials. The residence halls can accommodate 1,561 students. The current enrollment is 2,353 with a student-faculty ratio of 16 to 1.

Curriculum:

The College gives priority to teaching by continually adapting teaching techniques to meet student needs and by providing support programs f faculty development. The College's academic calendar is based on the semester system. Bachelor degrees are offered in the following areas: Accounting, Biology*, Business Administration, Business Education, Chemistry*, Criminal Justice, Elementary Education, English*, Exceptional Student Education, History, Hospitality management, Management, Mass Communication*, Mathematics*, Medical Technology, Modern Language*, Music*, Nursing, Physical Education, Political Science, Psychology, Religion and Philosophy*, Sociology, Social Studies Education and a Master's degree in Biology or Chemist Education.
*With or without teacher certification.

Financial:

Annual cost for tuition and fees is approximately $4,200 per semester living on campus and $2,650 living off campus. Nearly 91 percent of the students receive some type of financial aid through the College's various grants, scholarships, loans and employment assistance programs.

Bluefield State College
Bluefield, West Virginia 24701
(304) 327-4000

History:

Bluefield Colored Institute was founded in 1895 for African American students . The name was changed to Bluefield State Teachers College in 1931, and twelve years later was amended to Bluefield State College in recognition of the College's expanded mission and curricular offerings. During the early 1950s, Bluefield enrolled approximately 350 full-time students. The college integrated in 1954 and subsequently, curriculum offerings expanded. By the early 60s, Bluefield State had become a comprehensive four-year institution offering programs in arts and sciences, business, engineering technology and teacher education. Today, Bluefield State implements a variety of two- and four-year career-technical programs.

Location and Enrollment:

Located approximately 100 miles south of Charleston, Bluefield State College is the only four-year public college in West Virginia that serves its students entirely on a commuting basis. Enrollment consists of approximately 3,000 full-time and part-time students.

Curriculum:

Bachelor of Science Degrees are offered in Accountancy, Adolescent Education, Applied Science, Architectural Engineering Technology, Business Administration, Civil Engineering Technology, Computer Science, Criminal Justice Administration, Early/Middle Education, Electrical Engineering Technology, Mathematics, Mining Engineering Technology and Professional Nursing. Bachelor of Arts Degrees are offered in English, History, Regents Bachelor of Arts and Social Science. Associate of Science Degrees are offered in Applied Science (Lab Science), Architectural Engineering Technology, Computer Science, Engineering, General Business, General Education, Law Enforcement, Mechanical Engineering Technology, Radiologic Technology, Secretarial Science and Technical Nursing.

Financial:

Tuition and Fees are approximately $800 per semester for in-state students and $2,000 for out-of-state students. Forty-percent of all students and eight percent of full-time students including freshmen receive some form of financial aid.

Bowie State College
Bowie, Maryland 20715
(301) 464-6571

History:

Bowie State College, founded in 1865, has had a long-term commitment to provide for all its students, an equality of educational opportunities. Bowie has a strong emphasis on education for leadership and community service.

Location and Enrollment:

Bowie State College is located on a 280-acre campus off Interstate 197 and 450, and is centered on the outskirts of Washington, D.C. and Baltimore. The current enrollment at Bowie State College is approximately 4,500.

Curriculum:

Bachelor Degrees are offered in several areas: Anthropology/Sociology, Art, English, International Studies, Political Sciences, Psychology, Social Science, Speech/Theater, Biology, Business Administration, Music, Physical Education, Science, Early Childhood Education, Mathematics, Science Education, Social Work, Dual Degree Engineering, Foreign Languages, Art Education, Communications Media, Elementary Education, Journalism, Mathematics Education, Music Education, Nursing, Public Administration, Speech and Linguistics. Graduate Degrees are offered in Elementary Education, Counseling Psychology, Administrative Management, Business Administration, Public Administration, Elementary and Secondary School Administration, Reading Education, Secondary Education, Special Education.

Financial:

Approximate cost per year for in-state students is $3,754 if you choose to live on campus, and $1,368 for students who choose to live off campus. Out-of-state students costs range from $2,564 living off campus and $5,154 living on campus. The financial aid programs that Bowie State College participates in include: Other Race (minority) Grants, College Work Study, Pell Grants, Supplemental Education, Bank (related) Student Loans, Opportunity Grant and Various Scholarships.

Central State University
Wilberforce, Ohio 45384
(513) 376-6011

History:

Central State University was established in 1887 by the State of Ohio as a combined normal and industrial school. In 1941 the school became an independent, four-year institution.

Location and Enrollment:

Wilberforce is located 18 miles east of Dayton, Ohio and 50 miles northeast of Cincinnati, Ohio. The University is in a rural residential setting. The school owns 700 acres of land, 75 of which are main campus and there are 2 farms for outdoor education programs. The rest of the land is currently undeveloped. Current enrollment at the University is 3,266.

Curriculum:

Central State has a four-year Baccalaureate program in Manufacturing, Engineering requiring practical internships and course study in Industrial Technology, requiring mathematics, chemistry, physics and computerized design techniques. There are also a number of degrees available with areas of study in Business and Education. Cooperative Education is also available.

Financial:

The University participates in all Federal and State grant and loan programs, such as: College Work Study, Pell Grant, Ohio Instructional Grant, Supplemental Educational Opportunity Grant and Student Loan. Various institutional-based scholarships are available based on fulfillment of requirements. Tuition and fees depend on residency. Average costs per quarter for out-of-state residents is $3,625 on campus and $2,122 off campus. In-state residents pay $2,446 on-campus and $950 off-campus per quarter.

Cheyney University
Cheyney, Pennsylvania 19319
(215) 399-2275   1-800-243-9639

History:

Cheyney State is known as the oldest, historically black institution of
higher learning in the nation. Founded in 1837 and originally located in
Philadelphia, Cheyney moved to its present site in 1903. In 1921, the
University was purchased by the Commonwealth of Pennsylvania.
Today, Cheyney, along with 13 other state-owned universities, make up
the State System of Higher Education.

Location and Enrollment:

The campus is located on a 275-acre rural suburban site, just 24 miles
from Philadelphia. There is a bus service to the campus and train service
nearby. Student enrollment at Cheyney is approximately 1,800.

Curriculum:

Cheyney offers 39 majors including Business Administration, Education,
Communications, Math and Computer Sciences. Bachelor of Science
Degrees are also offered in Marine Science, Earth Science, Biology,
Chemistry and Anthropology. Graduate programs include: Elementary
Education, Industrial Arts Education, English Education, General
Science, Administration and Supervision, Special Education.

Financial:

Tuition scholarships are available in different academic areas. The
College requires students in need of financial aid to fill out a Form of
Eligibility in order to assess each situation and evaluate needs. The
programs available to students are as follows: Pell Grant, State
T.H.E.A.A. Grant, College Work Study, Supplemental Educational
Opportunity Grant and National Direct Student Loan. Various
scholarships are available in different academic areas. For residents,
Cheyney State students pay $3,489 including room and board per
semester. Non-resident boarding students pay $5,636 per semester.

Chicago State University
Chicago, Illinois 60628-1598
(312) 995-2513

History:

Established in 1867, Chicago State University has experienced a dramatic transformation of its student body over the past few decades. With emphasis on educational opportunities for inner-city students, this fully accredited, public, urban commuter institution has had an astounding 58 percent rise in enrollment over the last four years. The university has received wide-spread recognition for its model program that incorporates three principles: preparing and recruiting students through pre-college initiatives; retaining and graduating students through academic program improvement and safety nets; and providing students with opportunities for career and professional advancement through internships, graduate and professional study.

Location and Enrollment:

The 161 acre campus has nine contemporary buildings surrounded by a carefully preserved woodland setting. It is conveniently situated just 12 miles south of Chicago's Loop. Approximately 10,110 students are enrolled in 35 undergraduate and 14 graduate degree granting programs through the Colleges of Arts and Sciences, Business, Education, Nursing and Allied Health Professions.

Curriculum:

Bachelor of Arts, Bachelor of Science and Bachelor of Science in Education degrees are awarded in the following fields of study: Art, Biology, Chemistry, Computer Science, Criminal Justice, Economics, English, Geography, History, Mathematics, Music, Physics, Psychology, Sociology/Anthropology, Spanish , Speech, Accounting, Finance, Hotel and Restaurant Management, Information Systems Management, Marketing, Bilingual/Bicultural Education, Business Education, Early Childhood Education, Elementary Education, Nursing, Occupational Therapy, Health Information Administration. Master of Arts, Master of Science and Master of Science in Education degrees are also available. Special academic programs include Engineering Studies, Premedical Education and Minority biomedical Research.

Financial:

Current tuition and fees per semester for in-state students is $1,200. Cost for non-residents is approximately $3,200. Students have a vaireity of financial aid programs available.

Claflin College
Orangeburg, South Carolina 29115
(803) 534-2710 (803) 534-2710

History:

Claflin College was founded in 1869 to provide education primarily for people who were seriously in need of intellectual training and spiritual support. Its founders were humanitarians -- courageous men with vision. These qualities were interwoven in the "Philosophy of Claflin."

As one of the older four-year colleges in South Carolina, Claflin is a coeducational, private institution affiliated with the United Methodist Church.

Location and Enrollment:

The College is situated on 29 acres of land near the business district of Orangeburg, South Carolina and is 40 miles from the state's capital city, Columbia. Student enrollment ranges is 1,000.

Curriculum:

The College's academic calendar is based on the semester system. Claflin offers majors in a wide variety of disciplines -- from the humanities to the sciences. Students may pursue Bachelor of Arts or Bachelor of Science degrees with either a teaching or non-teaching option. This liberal arts college has academic programs such as computer science, religion and philosophy, art, business, sociology, music, chemistry and mathematics. One of Claflin's strengths is the individualized attention given to students. The faculty-student ratio is 1-to-17.

Financial:

Tuition, general fees, room and board will cost a student living on campus approximately $7,500 per year. For an off-campus student the tuition and general fees will cost approximately $5,000 per year. Financial Aid packages are available through a number of sources. Students must be accepted by the Office of Admissions before Financial Aid can be awarded.

Clark Atlanta University
Atlanta, Georgia 30314
(404) 880-8000

History:

Clark Atlanta University was formed in 1988 through the consolidation of
Atlanta University and Clark College. Clark Atlanta is one of only two
private historically black comprehensive universities in the nation. The
University is a member institution of the United Negro College Fund. It is
accredited by the Southern Association of Colleges and Schools, State of
Georgia Department of Education and the University Senate of the
Methodist Church. Members of the faculty are known for their warmth
and dedication to students. They bring the knowledge and experiences of
advanced degrees earned at renowned universities throughout the U.S.

Location and Enrollment:

One mile east of the campus lie the mirrored skyscrapers and modern
expressways of Atlanta, the world's next international city. Entertainment
abounds in the capitol of the Sunbelt. There are numerous cultural and
sporting activities. Enrolling about 5,000 undergraduate and graduate
students from forty states and fifty foreign countries, Clark Atlanta is one
the six colleges that make up the Atlanta University Consortium, the
largest consortium in the world of historically black learning centers.

Curriculum:

Clark Atlanta University is comprised of the School of Arts and Sciences
and professional Schools of Business Administration, Education, Library
and Information Studies and Social Work. The University offers courses
leading to: the Bachelor of Arts Degree in 33 majors including Art,
Business Administration, Education, English, Mass Media Arts, Physical
Education, Psychology and Speech Communication and Theater Arts;
the Bachelor of Science Degree in 10 majors including Allied Health,
Biology, Chemistry, Computer Science, Engineering, Mathematics and
Nutrition; the Bachelor of Social Work Degree; the Ph.D. Degree; the
Doctor of Education Degree; the Doctor of Arts Degree; the Educational
Specialist Degree and the Specialist in Library Services.

Financial:

Current tuition for students living on campus is approximately $10,000
per year and $7,000 for students living off campus. In addition, students
should allocate $250 per semester for books and personal expenses.

Coppin State College
Baltimore, Maryland 21216
(410) 383-5990

History:

Coppin State was founded in 1900 and today is a public, four-year, coeducational institution. The college is state supported and accredited by the Middle States Association of Colleges and Secondary Schools. The College has had a growing commitment to provide a quality education to all who wished to enroll and desire advancement.

Location and Enrollment:

The College is located in the urban/residential area of Northwest Baltimore, Maryland and is within 10 to 15 minutes from shopping. The campus is on 38 acres of land and is easily accessible by public transportation. Facilities include NCAA baseball and soccer fields; nine buildings including the College center for student activities and the which houses basketball courts, swimming pool, handball and racquetball courts, dance studio and weight room; the Grace Hill Jacobs Office/Classroom Building which houses a television studio and over 200 personal computers for students to use. Student enrollment at the college is 2,500 full-time and 300 part-time.

Curriculum:

Coppin College offers quality Bachelor Degrees in the following areas: Nursing (BSN), Mathematics, Computer Science, Management Science, Special Education, Elementary Education, Early Childhood Education, Biology, Chemistry, Criminal Justice, Applied Psychology, English, General Science, History, Adapted Physical Education, Social Science-Social Work, Philosophical Theology, Pre-Dentistry; Dual Degree, Pre-Engineering; dual degree, Pre-Pharmacy; dual degree, Pre-Med, Pre-Dental Hygiene, Pre-Physical Therapy and Pre-Law.

Financial:

Coppin State College is one of the least expensive institutions under the Board of Trustees of the State Universities and Colleges of Maryland. Tuition per semester is $1,297 for residents and $2,333 for non-residents. Room and board is approximately $2,270. To assist students, financial aid packages are available through grants, loans, state scholarships and work study opportunities.

Delaware State College
Dover, Delaware 19901
(302) 739-4917

History:

On May 15, 1891, the 58th General Assembly of the State of Delaware passed "An Act to Establish and Maintain a College for the Education of Colored Students in Agriculture and the Mechanic Arts" by virtue of the Second Morrill Act of Congress approved August 30, 1890. The Morrill Act of 1890 provided a permanent annual endowment of twenty-five thousand dollars ($25,000) for each land-grant college established under the provisions of the Morrill Act of 1862 and allowed a portion of the federal appropriation to be used for the endowment, support and maintenance of land grant colleges for Negro youths in states which maintained separate educational facilities. This legislation provided for the establishment of Delaware State College.

Location:

Delaware State College is located in Dover, Kent County, Delaware, 45 miles south of Wilmington on the Delmarva Peninsula. The campus is adjacent to U.S. Highway 13 which provides direct access to Norfolk, Virginia; Salisbury, Maryland; Wilmington, Delaware; Philadelphia, Pennsylvania; and Camden, New Jersey. The city of Dover is located on bus routes to major cities. Student population averages between 2,000-3,000.

Curriculum:

Delaware State College is a fully-accredited institution of higher education that grants the Master of Arts (M.A.) degree in education, Master of Business Administration (M.B.A.), Master of Social Work (M.S.W.), Master of Science in Biology and in Biology Education, Master of Science in Chemistry and in Applied Chemistry, Master of Science in Physics and in Physics Teaching, Master of Arts in Science Education, Bachelor of Arts (B.A.) degree, Bachelor of Science (B.S.) degree, and the Bachelor of Technology (B. Tech.) degrees.

Financial:

The approximate tuition and fee per semester for in-state students is $1,996 if commuting and $5,776 if living on-campus. Costs for out-of-state students is approximately $4,998 per year if living off-campus and $8,808 if boarding. Financial assistance at the College is made available through scholarship grants, loans and part-time employment opportunities. All funds are administered by the Office of Financial Aid.

Dillard University
New Orleans, Louisiana 70122
(504) 283-8822

History:

Dillard University's history dates back to more than a century. The parent Institutions, Straight College and New Orleans University were founded in 1869 and merged in 1930 to form one school named in honor of James Hardy Dillard,
a noted scholar and educator. Dillard University had the first nationally-accredited nursing program in Louisiana and established the first speech department at a black university.

Location and Enrollment:

Part of the pleasant experiences associated with attending Dillard is its location in New Orleans. The city is noted for its fine food and entertainment, with restaurants known all over the world and the kind of jazz that emanates from horns of music greats such as: Winton Marsalis, Pete Fountain and the late Louis Armstrong. Dillard serves more that 1,500 students from 39 states, the District of Columbia, three U.S. Territories and nine foreign countries.

Curriculum:

Dillard University offers courses and major fields of study in six academic divisions: Business, Natural Sciences, Education, Social Sciences, Nursing and Humanities. Degrees offered are the Bachelor of Arts, Bachelor of Science and Bachelor of Science in Nursing. Majors may be declared from a choice of 30 different areas of study. Double majors are also encouraged.

Financial:

The University makes every opportunity available to students to apply and receive some form of financial aid if needed. Financial aid is in the form of grants, scholarships, loans and the college work-study program. The tuition and fees for yearly study at Dillard are approximately $10,050. This amount covers room and board charges also. Students living off-campus can expect to pay $6,500.

District Of Columbia, University of the
Washington, D.C. 20004
(202) 282-3230

History:

The history of the University of the District of Columbia is at the same time very old and very new. It was founded in 1976 due to the consolidation of Washington's three outstanding institutions of higher learning -- the District of Columbia Teacher's College, Federal City College and Washington Technical Institute.

Location and Enrollment:

The University's location in the nation's capitol offers students access to cultural, intellectual and political activities unequalled anywhere in the United States. Opportunities for students to participate in the life of the community are enhanced by the University's commitment to involvement to involvement in the life and needs of the city. Total enrollment of the University is approximately 11,000.

Curriculum:

Within the University of the District of Columbia, are the Colleges of Business and Public Management, Education and Human Ecology, Engineering and Technology, Liberal and Fine Arts, Life Sciences and Physical Science. The University College serves as a point of entry for all first-time students. All students continue to be enrolled in the college until they have completed specific requirements in the associate and baccalaureate degree programs. The Division of Continuing Education coordinates the outreach programs of the University of the District of Columbia. The division provides opportunities for residents of the Washington Metropolitan area to obtain academic and technical education and training which may lead to upgrading of employment status etc.

Financial:

Undergraduate tuition for non-residents is $144 per credit hour; residents of the District of Columbia pay $144 per credit hour. Financial aid is available for eligible students. To be eligible to receive assistance from the various financial aid programs, a student must be enrolled on at least a half-time basis, in good academic standing (maintaining a 2.0 grade point average), in financial need and meet the Federal and University eligibility requirements. The application deadline for financial aid is March 15.

Edward Waters College
Jacksonville, Florida 32209
(904) 355-3030

History:

Edward Waters College is a historically black college founded in 1866 and is the oldest private Institution of higher education for blacks in the state of Florida. The College is a coeducational Institution affiliated with the African Methodist Church.

Location and Enrollment:

Edward Waters 20-acre campus is located in the urban development of Jacksonville, Florida. Ten buildings house the College's academic curriculum, information, facilities and knowledge. The College library contains approximately 109,000 volumes of a wide variety of information for the 750 students enrolled at the College.

Curriculum:

Edward Waters College is a four-year degree granting institution with Bachelor Degrees offered in: English, Biology, Chemistry, Mathematics, Business Administration, Criminal Justice, Health and Physical Education, Social Science/Social Work, Elementary Education, Public Administration, Religion and Philosophy, Accounting, Computer Information, Office Communications. The College has 15 programs in which the choice of a major may be decided.

Financial:

The approximate cost per semester at the college is $3,665, covering tuition, fees, room and board. For students living off-campus the cost is $1,785 per semester. The College offers various types of financial aid and is decided upon by two important factors, individual need and academic potential. Edward Waters College offers the following forms of financial aid to its students: loans, grants, scholarships and on-campus employment.

Elizabeth City State University
Elizabeth City, North Carolina 27909
(919) 335-3305

History:

Elizabeth City State University, founded in 1891, was initially created as a normal school for the purpose of "teaching and training teachers" of the "colored" race to teach in the "common schools" ofNorth Carolina. The school moved to its present site in 1912 with a second purpose given, the training of elementary school principals for rural and city schools. The only historically black, four-year institution in northeastern North Carolina, Elizabeth City State University provides a liberal arts education, as well as specialized preparation, and is open to students of diverse backgrounds and culture who seek a genuine education. In 1992, the University began its second century of providing education.

Location and Enrollment:

The University's 829-acre campus is located in Elizabeth City, North Carolina near the mouth of the Pasquotank River. The University is a 50-minute drive from the beautiful Outer Banks and some of the world's best beaches. United States Highways 17 and 158 make the city and University easily accessible by automobile and bus routes from all points. Student population is approximately 2,100.

Curriculum:

The University offers degrees in the Bachelor of Arts and the Bachelor of Science in disciplines such as Geology, Biology, General Science, Medical Technology, Industrial Arts and Military Science. There are also specialized Bachelor degrees offered in Arts and Science for Education and Teacher Certification. Cooperative Education is also available.

Financial:

Tuition is $722 a semester for in-state students, and $3,231 for out-of-state students living off campus. Room and board is approximately $1,431. Financial aid is available in the form of: grants, scholarships, loans and work study programs.

Fayetteville State University
Fayetteville, North Carolina 28301-4298
(919) 486-1111

History:

Excellence in achievement is the foundation on which Fayetteville State University was formed in 1867. Recognized for its broad spectrum in the educational process, as well as a long list of faculty achievements and state-of-the-art facilities, Fayetteville State University's history can be traced back to a one-building school built 120 years ago on two lots purchased for $136. Today, 156 acres and 36 buildings provide a balanced program of activities for the moral, cultural and physical development of its students, as well as social and recreational activities sponsored by various departments.

Location and Enrollment:

The University is ideally located in the fourth largest urban population center in North Carolina, a short distance from the downtown area, Fayetteville Municipal Airport, and three main highways. Full-time student enrollment is 3,800.

Curriculum:

The University's academic structure is characterized by three major units: The College of Arts and Sciences, The School of Education and the School of Business and Economics. Many degrees are offered within these units, including Speech Therapy, Political Science and Business Education. Graduate Degrees are available in Elementary Education, Special Education, and Education Administration. Weekend and evening college offers working men and women an opportunity to continue and complete their college education by receiving a regular, relevant degree curriculum.

Financial:

The estimated annual cost for a non-boarding resident is $1,370 and for a boarding resident, $3,926; the cost for a non-residents living off-campus is $7,442 and a boarding non-resident is $9,992. Financial aid is available to qualified students and students enrolled on at least a half-time basis. Students must apply for assistance.

**Fisk University
Nashville, Tennessee 37203
(615) 329-8500**

History:

Fisk University's foundations were laid in October, 1865. After the Civil
War, three agents of the American Missionary Association of New York
(now a part of the United Church of Christ) established in Nashville the
only school in the United States dedicated "to the education and training
of young women and men irrespective of color." The new opening of the
institution took place on January 9, 1866, and was named Fisk School in
honor of General Fisk. The corporate charter was signed on August
12,1897 when the idea of the Liberal Arts University was conceived and
the name was changed to Fisk University.

Location and Enrollment:

Fisk's campus is listed on the National Register of Historical Places. The
40-acre campus is located in Nashville, Tennessee, the capital city of the
state. Student enrollment has risen steadily in recent years. The current
enrollment is 1,000 students. As a percentage of enrollment, more
minority students from Fisk go on to achieve a Ph.D., degree than those
students from other colleges in the United States.

Curriculum:

Baccalaureate Degrees are offered in Art, Biology, Chemistry, Dramatics
and Speech, Economics, English, History, Mathematics, Music, Physics,
Political Science, Religion and Philosophy, Sociology, French
Management, Spanish, Health Care Administration Planning, Psychology
and Music Education. Graduate Degrees are offered in Chemistry,
Physics, Psychology and Sociology.

Financial:

Average costs per year at the University are estimated at $6,240 for
tuition and fees; $3,755 for room and board. Nearly half the student body
at Fisk University receive some type of financial assistance in the form of
grants, loans, scholarships or work-study programs.

Florida A&M University
Tallahassee, Florida 32307
(904) 599-3000

History:

Florida A&M (Agricultural and Mechanical) University was founded in 1887 and is a state-assisted rather than state-supported Institution. Although Florida A&M is a predominately black university, the curriculum has been designed to meet academic needs as well as social and developmental needs of all its students regardless of race, color or creed and this has been a standing commitment of the College throughout the decades.

Location and Enrollment:

The University covers 419 acres of land situated in the northwest panhandle of the fast growing urban area of Tallahassee, Florida with a population of 100,000. The school is located 30 miles from the Georgia state line and can be reached from interstate I-10 E or I-10 W or from Georgia 319. The student population at Florida A&M is approximately 10,000 students.

Curriculum:

The School of Business and Industry at the college has received national recognition for its innovative approach to education with its graduates distributed in major companies throughout the country. Bachelor Degrees are offered in over 50 undergraduate programs and the Graduate Degree programs consist of Adult and Continuing Education, Architecture, Applied Social Sciences, Business Administration, Business, Commerce and Distributive Education, Business Management, Community/School Psychology, Educational Administration, Educational Supervision, General Elementary Education, English Education, Industrial Arts Vocational and Technical Education, Mathematics Education, Pharmacy, Physical Education, Science Education, General Secondary Education, Social Studies Education, Student Personnel (Counseling and Guidance).

Financial:

The cost of an education at Florida A&M per semester for Florida residents is approximately $875. Non-residents pay approximately $2,275 per semester for tuition and fees. Room and board for both residents and non-residents is on average about $1,400 per semester. Financial Aid is available to students based on need and academic abilities.

Florida Memorial College
Miami, Florida 33054
(305) 625-4141

History:

Florida Memorial College was founded in 1879. It is one of the oldest colleges in Florida and was first located near the historic Suwannee River at Live Oaks as the Florida Baptist Institute for Negroes. In 1968, the Institute was moved to its present site. Florida Memorial is a residential college, centered in one of America's best known cities.

Location and Enrollment:

Florida Memorial is convenient to all of Miami. The Palmetto Expressway link is close by, as are the I-95 and Turnpike interchanges. As a tourist attraction, Miami offers a number of free things to do, as well as, the pop, jazz concerts, club entertainment and professional sporting events. Student population is approximately 1,850.

Curriculum:

Florida Memorial is divided into six divisions: (1) Airway Science offers a Bachelor of Science degree; (2) Business and Economics offers Bachelor of Science and Bachelor of Arts degrees; (3) Education offers Bachelor of Science in elementary and secondary education; (4) Humanities offers three major areas: Language, Fine Arts, Religion and Philosophy; (5) Natural Sciences and Mathematics and (6) Social Science offers Bachelor of Science degrees. The Institution operates on the semester system. Military studies are also offered in Aerospace Studies and Military Science.

Financial:

The cost per semester for on-campus students is $3,850 and for off-campus students is $2,375. Financial aid is available and packages are made up for students based on need and academic qualifications. The amount of aid is individualized by information supplied by each student.

Fort Valley State College
Fort Valley, Georgia 31030
(912) 825-6307

History:

Established in 1890, chartered in 1896, and made a four-year state supported institution by the University System of Georgia in 1939 when The Fort Valley Normal and Industrial School and the State Teachers and Agriculture College services were consolidated in Fort Valley, Georgia as The Fort Valley State College. The first four-year college class was graduated in 1941, consisting of 21 students. In 1947, the Institution was authorized by the University system to offer graduate programs. In 1949, the state legislature made FVSC Georgia's 1890 Land Grant College.

Location and Enrollment:

Geographically situated in the center of the state, the College is less than two hours away from Atlanta and 30 miles from Macon. The Institution has a student/teacher ratio of 14 to 1, with an average class size of 25. Current enrollment is nearly 2,200.

Curriculum:

An extensive and up-to-date curriculum is the rule, not the exception at Fort Valley State. The College offers Bachelor of Arts and Bachelor of Science Degrees in a wide variety of majors including Agriculture, Education and Home Economics. Graduate Degree programs offered in Elementary Education, Mental Health Counseling, Guidance and Counseling, and Vocational Rehabilitation. A dual degree program is open to students with a major in Mathematics, Physics or Chemistry. The student will attend the College for three years and Georgia Tech two. Upon completion of the program the student will receive a Bachelor of Science Degree from the College and a Bachelor's Degree in Engineering or Technical Field from Georgia Tech.

Financial:

Tuition per quarter is $1,412 for residents and $2,233 for non-residents living on-campus. Cost for off-campus living is $592 for residents and $1,513 for non-residents. Scholarships and financial aid are awarded on the basis of need, as well as merit. Financial aid comes through scholarships, grants, loans, and work/study opportunities. Applicants should apply in advance or registration.

Grambling State University
Grambling, Louisiana 71245
(318) 274-2435

History:

Founded in 1901, Grambling State University has had a mission which focuses on Undergraduate, Graduate and Professional degrees. Today, Grambling State University is a four-year, coeducational college.

Location and Enrollment:

The 380-acre campus of Grambling State University is located in the urban city of Grambling, Louisiana. Seventy-four buildings house the University's facilities. The library contains over 100,000 volumes packed with educational information. The current enrollment at the University consist of 7,000 students.

Curriculum:

The Institution offers a variety of graduate and undergraduate degree programs in areas such as Communication Disorders, Nursing, Social Welfare, Child Care, Public Administration, Criminal Justice, Sports, Special Development Education (the only program of its kind in the country), International Business and Trade and Business Administration. Baccalaureate Degrees have over 50 major program options to choose from. Graduate Degree programs offer Biology, Early Childhood Education, Elementary Education, Sports Administration, Sociology, Reading, Guidance, Special Education, Liberal Studies and Developmental Education. Grambling offers over 100 degrees in a variety of disciplines and offers Associate, Bachelors, Masters, Specialist and Doctoral degrees within its two schools and four colleges. Grambling also offers a joint Engineering Program with Louisiana Technical University.

Financial:

Tuition per semester is approximately $1,044 for in-state students. and $1,919 for out-of-state students. Room and board for is $1,400 per semester. Grambling offers the following types of financial aid: scholarships, grants, loans and employment.

Hampton University
Hampton, Virginia 23668
(804) 727-5000

History:

In 1868, Hampton Normal and Agricultural Institute was founded by
General Samuel Chapman Armstrong. That name was shortened in
1930 to Hampton Institute. In 1984, Hampton's Board of Trustees
established Hampton University. Today, the University is the parent
institution and includes Hampton Institute as the Undergraduate college,
a Graduate college and a College of Continuing Education. Hampton's
commitment to excellence has been and will always remain in the
forefront of its purpose.

Location and Enrollment:

Located on an old historic Virginia peninsula, Hampton's beauty is
reflected in the waters of Hampton Roads, on which it borders. Hampton
University is served by both Norfolk International Airport and Patrick
Henry Airport of Newport News. Both are equal distances from the
campus and provide direct limousine service. Enrollment at Hampton is
approximately 5,700 students from 42 states and 6 foreign countries.

Curriculum:

The University calendar is divided into two semesters of approximately
fifteen weeks of classes and a summer session. Bachelor Degrees are
offered in the undergraduate programs at Hampton Institute which lie in
the School of Arts and Letters (Division of Arts and Humanities), School
of Business, School of Education, School of Pure and Applied Sciences
and the School of Nursing. The graduate program at Hampton
University, leading to the Masters Degree, seeks to meet the needs of
the students who wish to pursue their training beyond the undergraduate
level in 9 different areas of study.

Financial:

Hampton University will make every effort to see that no qualified
candidate is refused admission because of lack of funds. The University
offers a number of grants, loans, scholarships and work-study
opportunities from federal, state, and private sources. Applications for
financial aid should be sent as early as possible. Annual cost for tuition
and fees for is approximately $7,350. Students requesting room and
board should add an additional $3,350. Books not included.

Harris-Stowe State College
St. Louis, Missouri 63103
(314) 533-3366

History:

Harris Teachers College, established in 1857 as a normal school for white students, became the first public teacher education institution west of the Mississippi River. A second predecessor institution was Stowe Teachers College which began in 1890 as a normal school for black future teachers of elementary schools. The St. Louis Public School System merged them in 1954 and in 1979, Harris-Stowe College became the newest member of the State system of public higher education.

Location and Enrollment:

The college is located at the hub of Metropolitan St. Louis, close to many major corporations, governmental agencies and nationally recognized cultural and educational resources. Current enrollment is 2,000 students.

Curriculum:

Harris-Stowe State College offers two broad degree program emphasis: (1) teacher education, leading to State of Missouri teacher certification and (2) urban education specialist education - a non-teaching public service degree program. The teacher education programs include majors in the following main areas: Early Childhood Education, Elementary School Education and Middle School/Junior High School Education. The Urban Education Specialist Education degree program has only one major. It is an innovation in American higher education in that it prepares at the baccalaureate level a new career specialist prepared to successfully confront today's educational and societal problem from a humanistic perspective. Since all of these undergraduate degree programs are professional in their emphasis; they all have well-defined professional curricula which are concentrated at the junior and senior levels.

Financial:

Current tuition and fees are $59 per credit hour for residents and $116 per credit hour for non residents. Fees are assessed each semester and are published prior to the beginning of each semester.

Huston-Tillotson College
Austin, Texas 78702
(512) 505-3000

History:

Huston-Tillotson College, founded in 1876, is a coeducational, Liberal Arts Institution supported by the Board of Education and the United Methodist Church along with the United Church of Christ through the United Missionary Association. The College has a history of providing its student body as well as faculty members the opportunity for intelligent and creative participation to develop and maintain certain standards of excellence in scholarship, character and the ability of self-expression.

Location and Enrollment:

The College campus is located on 23 acres of land in East Austin, the capital city of Texas with a population of over 500,000 people. Student population at Huston-Tillotson averages 500-1,000.

Curriculum:

The College offers undergraduate majors in Accounting, Computer Science, Economics, Finance/Banking, Marketing, Mathematics, Business Administration and Education, Industrial Administration and Hotel/Restaurant Management. Baccalaureate Degrees offered include Accounting, Biology, Business Administration, Chemistry, Economics, English, Government, Hotel and Restaurant Management, Industrial Relations and Personnel Management, Marketing, Mathematics, Physical Education and Recreation, Sociology, Teacher Education, Business Education, Computer Science, Finance, History and Music.

Financial:

The approximate cost per semester at the college include $2,520 for tuition and fees and $1,725 for room and board. Financial aid at the college is offered to all eligible students depending on need as well as academic performance. Approximately 70 percent of the student body receive some form of financial aid assistance in the form of grants, loans, on-campus or off-campus employment and scholarships based also on academic performance.

Howard University
Washington, D.C. 20059
(202) 806-6100

History:

Founded as a private university in 1867 by an Act of the U.S. Congress,
the University is named after General Oliver Otis Howard, commissioner
of the Freedmen's Bureau. While Howard University has always
embraced persons of all colors, religions, creeds and national origins, its
historical mission entrusted to it the education of newly emancipated
slaves and their descendants. It is that group of persons whom the
University primarily serves. Today, Howard University is the only
comprehensive university in the country with a predominantly black
constituency. It is often called the "mecca" because of the leadership
roles its faculty, students and alumni have historically played in the
political, scientific, intellectual and artistic area as of this country.

Location and Enrollment:

Howard University is located in one of the most cosmopolitan cities in the
world, Washington, D.C. Its reputation as the power center of the world
gives students an opportunity for first-hand observation and participation
in the political process. Howard students, numbering approximately
12,000, come from all over the nation and more than 90 countries.

Curriculum:

Howard University consists of many schools, such as: the Colleges of
Allied Health Sciences, Dentistry, Fine Arts, Liberal Arts, Medicine,
Pharmacy and Pharmacal Sciences, and Nursing, and the Schools of
Architecture and Planning, Business and Public Administration,
Communications, Education, Engineering, Human Ecology, Law, Social
Work, the Divinity School, the Graduate School of Arts and Sciences.
These schools and colleges offer degree programs in more than 200
specialized subjects.

Financial:

Tuition and fees for undergraduate students are $3,767; room and board
ranges between $1,900-$2,400 depending on accommodations. Tuition
for graduate and professional programs are somewhat higher. Howard
University's Financial Aid Program provides assistance in the form of
scholarships, loans, grants and part-time employment.

Howard University College of Medicine
Washington, DC 20059
(202) 806-6100

History:

Howard University College of Medicine was founded in 1868 and today the College takes pride in its long and illustrious history of training students to become competent and compassionate physicians providing health care in medically undeserved communities.

Location/Enrollment:

Howard University's College of Medicine is located on the 75-acre campus of Howard University, which is situated in the urban center of Washington. The College of Medicine is just a fraction of the 67 buildings that comprise the Institution's facilities. Howard University's College of Medicine enrolls up to 100 new students each year. The enrollment represents about 25 to 30 states and several African and Caribbean countries are usually represented.

Curriculum:

The academic programs of the College of Medicine are designed to prepare students to provide competent and compassionate service to their communities and the world. The traditional curriculum of the College of Medicine is a four-year program. In required courses, students are presented the essential knowledge and skills necessary for the practice of medicine.

Financial:

The tuition of the College of Medicine is $9,500. However, fees and other expenses will determine end costs. About 85 percent of the students enrolled in the College of Medicine receive some sort of financial aid. Financial aid awards are based on an analysis of the student's needs and academic ability. Financial aid applicants are required to file the Financial Aid Form (FAF) of the College Scholarship service.

InterDenominational Theological Center
Atlanta, Georgia 30314
(404) 577-7709

History:

Some of the major objectives that have been with the Interdenominational Theological Center since its founding in 1958, have been to accomplish the following: -to orient persons to the significance of the total program of theological education for ministry; -to increase knowledge of the Christian faith and competence in ministry; -to enhance understanding of the relevance of the Christian faith for ministry in the contemporary world; -to become cognizant of the academic worth of the Black experience and the needs of the Black witnessing community.

Location and Enrollment:

The size of the campus at the Interdenominational Theological Center is 10 acres, with 13 buildings comprising the Institution's facilities. The library carries approximately 53,744 volumes of books. The residential halls at the college can accommodate 800 students. The current student population at the College is 331.

Curriculum:

The center offers a four-year baccalaureate program in Religion/Theology, Christian Education and Church Music, and doctoral degrees in Religion/Theology and Pastoral Counseling. The center is known for its popularity in having one of the best field education programs of all seminaries in the United States. Graduate Degrees are given in cooperation with three seminaries. The Graduate titles are as follows: Master of Divinity, Master of Religious Education, Doctor of Divinity and Doctor of Sacred Theology. The Center graduates one-half of all African-American chaplains and the largest number of African-American female seminarians of any institution in the country.

Financial:

Tuition at the center is $2,000 per semester and $1,465 for room and board. There are approximately 90 percent of the total student body that receive financial aid in the form of loans, grants or scholarships.

Jackson State University
Jackson, Mississippi 39217
(601) 968-2121

History:

Jackson State University, founded in 1877 as a coeducational institution, currently is maintained by the State of Mississippi. The University is controlled by a Board of Trustees of Institutions of Higher Learning, appointed by the governor. The University is also supported by legislative appropriations supplemented by student fees, federal and private grants.

Location and Enrollment:

Jackson State University is located in Jackson, Mississippi, the state capital as well as the largest city in the state. Jackson is the geographical, political, industrial and cultural center of the state. The population of the metropolitan area of Jackson consists of an estimated 415,000. The current student enrollment of Jackson State University is approximately 8,000.

Curriculum:

The academic programs of the university are organized into the University College, the Honors College and five schools. These schools--School of Education, School of Business, School of Liberal Arts, School of Science and Technology, and the Graduate School--offer 40 bachelors, 30 masters, 10 specialist in education degree programs and the only Doctoral Degree program in Early Childhood Education in the state.

Financial:

Tuition per semester is $1,115 for residents and $2,232 for non-residents. Room and board is $1,300 per semester. Approximately 70 to 75 percent of the students at the college receive some form of financial aid. Jackson State makes available to each student the option for a financial aid package. Programs available at the college include: scholarships, grants, loans and employment in various forms.

Jarvis Christian College
Hawkins, Texas 75765
(903) 769-2174

History:

Since its founding in 1912, the opportunity for education in an environment which provides assistance has been a mainstay of the Jarvis Christian College experience. Throughout the years, demanding expectations of sustained performance has manifested itself within a climate of genuine understanding and concern for the diverse educational backgrounds and career goals of Jarvis students. The expectations coupled with concern are the basis of the personalized education you will find at Jarvis.

Location and Enrollment:

Jarvis Christian College is located on U.S. Highway 80 in the colorful, pined wooded area if East Texas in Hawkins, Texas. A quiet rural, and rustic beauty prevails enabling students to appreciate God's gift of the high quality of fresh, clean air, and enjoy an atmosphere conductive to study. Jarvis is midway between Dallas, Texas and Shreveport, Louisiana (approximately 100 miles) situated approximately 25 miles north of Tyler, Texas and 25 miles west of Longview. The student/teacher ratio at Jarvis Christian College is 11-1, with a total student population of 500.

Curriculum:

Degree programs are offered in the categories of: Bachelor of Arts, Associates of Arts, Bachelor of Science in Education, Bachelor of Science and Bachelor of Business Administration. The requirements for the Bachelors Degree are structured to ensure that students ascertain both depth and diversity in their studies.

Financial:

Tuition per semester including room and board averages approximately $3,585. Jarvis has one of the most comprehensive programs of financial aid assistance available anywhere. Most financial assistance is based upon need and every attempt is made to see that no admissible student eliminates Jarvis Christian College for financial reasons. Such aid may be received in the form of direct scholarships, grants, loans, college work study jobs or a combination consisting of two or more of these forms of financial assistance.

Johnson C. Smith University
Charlotte, North Carolina 28216-5398
(704) 378-1000

History:

As one of the nation's oldest, historically Black Universities, Johnson C. Smith University has compiled a 125-year legacy of achievement and excellence. Today, Johnson C. Smith remains a select liberal arts college in the classical tradition. Quite simply, Johnson C Smith University is one of the oldest and most progressive historically Black Universities. Founded in 1867, the University has an unparalleled record of achievement, producing many of this nation's black leaders.

Location and Enrollment:

Located on a 100-acre, tree-lined campus, just a diploma cap's throw from downtown Charlotte, Johnson C. Smith University is home for over 1,200 students who thrive in an environment ideal for personal, social and intellectual growth. There's a magical blend of urban and pastoral through the convenient location of major highways I-77 and I-85. The student-faculty ratio of 17-1 assures time focused on the needs of individual students.

Curriculum:

The University is a liberal arts institution offering course work leading to a Bachelor of Arts, Bachelor of Science and Bachelor of Social Work degree. Twenty-six programs of study offer a wide variety of educational opportunities. Within four major divisions-the Humanities; the Social Sciences; Education, Physical Education, Health and Psychology; and Mathematics and Sciences-a number of specialized programs may be followed, including Pre-Med, Pre-Dental and Pre-Law. In addition, some exciting new cooperative programs have taken shape, combining the assets of various campuses from surrounding universities.

Financial:

In order for all students to have the opportunity for a quality education, the University offers a wide variety of financial aid programs which include federally funded programs such as Supplementary Education Opportunity Grants, Pell, and Perkins Loans. Also available are aid from the state and scholarships. Total cost for students is approximately $8,900 a year living on campus and $6,700 off campus.

Kentucky State University
Frankfort, Kentucky 40601
(502) 227-6813; (800) 633-9415 Kentucky
(800) 325-1716 Outside Kentucky

History:

Kentucky State University was founded in 1886
as a liberal studies, public institution which
has always emphasized on quality and individualization. Kentucky State
University is truly serious about a quality education.

Location and Enrollment:

The University is located on the western edge of the Bluegrass region in
Kentucky's capitol city, Frankfort (with a population of 27,500). The
University is located on Interstate 64, less than an hour drive from
Interstates 71, 65 and 75, the Bluegrass Parkway and the Mountain
Parkway. Frankfort is 25 miles west of Lexington and 50 miles east of
Louisville (Kentucky's two largest cities). Bus transportation is available
to and from both cities. The total enrollment at the college is 2,700
students with 2,500 undergraduates.

Curriculum:

Degree programs offered are as follows: Mathematics, Music, Art,
Biology, Business Administration, Business Education, Chemistry, Child
Development/Family Relations, Computer Science, Criminal Justice,
Dietetics/Food Service Management, Drafting and Design Technology,
Electronics, Early Elementary Education, English, History, Liberal
Studies, Medical Technology, Nursing, Office Administration, Physical
Education, Political Science, Psychology, Public Administration, Public
Affairs, Social Studies, Social Work, Sociology, Studio Art,
Textiles/Clothing/Merchandising. Pre-Professional study: Community
Health, Cytotechnology, Dentistry, Engineering, Law, Medicine, Nuclear
Medicine Technology, Optometry, Physical Therapy, and Veterinary
Medicine.

Financial:

The costs per year at Kentucky State University are $2,250 per semester
for out-of-state and $750 per semester for in-state students. Room and
board is $1,350 per semester. Eligibility for financial assistance is based
on demonstrated financial need, scholastic ability, useful talent, training
and experience. More than 50 types of academic, special talent, and
athletic scholarships are offered.

Knoxville College
Knoxville, Tennessee 39721
(615) 524-6500

History:

Founded in 1875, Knoxville College is a coeducational, liberal arts institution affiliated with the United Presbyterian Church (USA), and is accredited by the Southern Association of Colleges and Schools.

Location and Enrollment:

Situated in urban Knoxville, Tennessee, the College campus has 32 acres and 22 buildings. The College library consists of approximately 77,000 volumes. The student enrollment at Knoxville College is approximately 1,000 students. The Morristown campus has approximately 150 students.

Curriculum:

Knoxville's academic calendar is based on the semester system with degrees offered in the Bachelor of Science, the Bachelor of Arts and the Associate of Arts. Undergraduate majors include: Art, Biological Sciences, Business and Commerce, Education, English and Literature, Foreign Languages, History and Cultures, Mathematics, Music, Physical Sciences, Psychology and Social Sciences. Special programs are offered in Cooperative Education; three/two Liberal Arts and a Dual Degree Engineering Program are in affiliation with the University of Tennessee, Knoxville. Programs are also offered in Air Force and Army ROTC. Computer literacy is required of all graduates, making Knoxville College one of the few private, four-year institutions in the country to have such a requirement.

Financial:

The tuition cost per year at Knoxville for residents is approximately $5,200 for tuition, room and board and fees. The out-of-state student pays approximately $9,000. The average student at the College receives some type of financial aid. Knoxville College offers the following financial aid programs: National Direct Student Loans, Grant-in-Aid, College Work Study, Academic Award, Performance Award (Sport and Music), Grants, Basic Education Opportunity Grant.

Lane College
Jackson, Tennessee 38301
(901) 426-7500

History:

Lane College was founded in 1882 by the Colored Methodist Episcopal Church of America. It was first established as a high school under the direction of Bishop Isaac Lane, with his daughter as principal. The high school became Lane Institute in 1883. Its first president, Reverend T. F. Saunders, served from 1887 to 1903. The present name of Lane College was received in 1895.

Location and Enrollment:

Lane College is located in the northeast section of Jackson, Tennessee, nearly mid-point between the cities of Memphis and Nashville. The 15-acre campus, within walking distance of Jackson's downtown area, offers an attractive blend of contemporary and traditional architecture. Five of the 16 buildings, which spread across the College grounds, have been included in the National Register of Historic Places. Lane College has a 15-to-1 student/teacher ratio. This assures a more academic, personalized instruction. The approximate enrollment is 800.

Curriculum:

The College calendar is based on the semester system with Bachelor Degrees offered in Art and Science. Majors are as follows: Biology, Business, Chemistry, Communications, Elementary Education, English, Computer Science, Engineering (offered in cooperation with Tennessee State University), Math/Computer Science, Mathematics, Music, Health, Physical Education, Recreation, History, Religion, Sociology. Pre-professional programs: Health Sciences and Nursing.

Financial:

The average tuition cost with room and board is about $3,814 per semester. The financial assistance program is designed to supplement family and student resources. Funds are provided by Lane College, the U.S. Department of Education, state and agencies and many other foundations. The following programs are available: Pell, Supplemental Educational Opportunity Grant, Tennessee Student Assistance Award, Guaranteed Student Loan/Plus Loan, College Work Study, Academic Scholarships.

Langston University
Langston, Oklahoma 73050
(405) 466-2231

History:

Langston University was founded in 1887 as a four-year college and is historically known as an integral part of Oklahoma's State System of Higher Education. The University is also a land-grant college. The mission at Langston University is to provide urban residents with an opportunity to train to their fullest potential for working, living and coping with the realities of urban life.

Location and Enrollment:

Langston University is located on 40 acres in Langston, Oklahoma. The college is situated in an urban area of the city and Oklahoma City is only 40 miles away. The total student population of the college is nearly 3,800 with a student/teacher ratio of 23 to 1.

Curriculum:

The academic calendar at Langston University rotates on the semester system. Degrees offered include: Associate of Arts, Associate of Science, Bachelor of Arts and Bachelor of Science. Undergraduate majors include Agriculture (Animal Science, Agriculture Economics), Art (Commercial), Biological Sciences (Biology), Business and Commerce (Business Administration and Management, Secretarial Studies), Communications, Computer Science and Systems Analysis (Data Processing), Education (Elementary, Music, Art), Home Economics (Clothing and Textiles), Social Sciences (Sociology and Social Work). Special programs offered are the Accelerated Program, Cooperative Education, Independent Study and Honors Program.

Financial:

The cost of attending Langston College varies from student to student depending on the number of credit hours. The tuition cost for in-state students is approximately $1,000 per semester and for out-of-state students, $2,770. Room and board is $1,250. Financial aid is available at the college and 75 percent of the total student body receives some type of assistance through scholarships, loans, grants and/or employment.

LeMoyne-Owen College
Memphis, Tennessee 38126
(901) 774-9090

History:

Founded in 1870 as a four-year, coeducational, private college, LeMoyne-Owen College has had an up-standing commitment of providing students with the opportunity to achieve the highest education possible combining liberal arts and sciences with career preparation. The college is accredited by the Southern Association of Colleges and Schools.

Location and Enrollment:

The LeMoyne-Owen College is situated in Memphis, Tennessee between Mississippi and Belvue. The college can be reached from Interstate 240. Memphis is one of the biggest cities in Tennessee with Nashville as state capitol. The College enrollment of full-time students consists of over 1,600.

Curriculum:

The College's curriculum is based on the trimester system with Bachelor Degrees offered in Art, Economics, English, History, Humanities, Political Science, Social Work, Sociology, Business Administration, Accounting, Biology, Chemistry, Elementary Education, Health and Physical Education, Mathematics, Natural Science, Physics and Social Science. Bachelor Degrees are titled as follows: Bachelor of Business Administration, Bachelor of Science and Bachelor of Arts.

Financial:

The total tuition cost per semester is $2,250 and room and board is $1,800. Financial aid is available for students in the form of grants, loans and employment. The financial aid package is available to students who meet certain requirements outlined on the applications.

Lincoln University
Jefferson City, Missouri 65101
(314) 681-5000

History:

At the close of the American Civil War, the soldiers and officers of the sixty-second United States Colored Infantry-stationed at Fort McIntosh, Texas, but composed principally of Missourians-decided to establish Lincoln Institute, with the following stipulations: (1) The institution shall be designed for the special benefit of the freed blacks, (2) It shall be located in the state of Missouri, and (3) Its fundamental aim shall be to combine study and labor. Members of the Sixty-second Colored Infantry contributed $5,000 to open the school and they appealed for help to the Sixty-fifth Colored Infantry, which gave $1,324.50. Lincoln University moved to its present site in 1869, and in 1954, opened it's doors to any qualified person who wished to enroll.

Location and Enrollment:

The University's 137-acre campus is located "on the hill", in Jefferson City, the capitol of Missouri. The University is within three hours from Kansas City and St. Louis. More than 4,000 full time students attend Lincoln University, with 15 percent being from out-of-state and 7 percent international.

Curriculum:

The University is divided into two semesters. The University is also divided into two main colleges, The College of Arts and Sciences and The College of Professional Studies. In addition there is an Office of Graduate Studies and continuing education. Six undergraduate degrees are offered, Bachelor of Arts, Bachelor of Science, Bachelor of Science in Education, Bachelor of Music, Associate of Arts, Associate of Applied Sciences.

Financial:

Tuition/fees for a nine month academic year total $2,035 in state and $4,635 out of state. Room and board per year totals $2,700. The primary cost of education lies with the student and/or their family. There is a wide variety of financial aid programs available to supplement the student in the form of grants, loans, employment and scholarships.

**Lincoln University
Lincoln, Pennsylvania 19352
(215) 932-8300**

History:

Lincoln University is a non-sectarian, coeducational, state-related four-year liberal arts institution. Founded in 1854, Lincoln is the oldest college in the United States to have as its original purpose the higher education of black youth. Since 1866, it has provided a superior liberal arts education for students of all races and nationalities.

Location and Enrollment:

The campus is surrounded by the rolling farmlands and hills of Southern Chester County in Pennsylvania. It is located on Pennsylvania Route 131, approximately 45 miles south of Philadelphia, 25 miles west of Wilmington, Delaware, and 55 miles north of Baltimore, Maryland. Current enrollment is approximately 1,300.

Curriculum:

Lincoln University offers four-year programs leading to the Undergraduate Degrees of Bachelor of Arts and Bachelor of Science. Majors available to students range from Accounting and Biology to Sociology/Anthropology and Therapeutic Recreation. Professional programs in Law, Medicine, and Nursing are also offered. Two-year programs leading to Associate of Arts Degree are offered in Business Administration, Computer Science, Early Childhood Education, Spanish and Recreation Leadership.

Financial:

Tuition for residents of Pennsylvania is $6,687 with room and board. Out-of-state students pay $8,447. Financial aid awards are based on need. Over 90% of students at Lincoln receive some type of financial aid. Aid is awarded in the form of packages which may include scholarships, federal grants, state grants, Perkin's Loans, Guaranteed Student Loans, and College Work Study Program Awards.

**Livingstone College
Salisbury, North Carolina 28144
(704) 638-5500**

History:

Supported largely by the African Methodist Episcopal Zion Church,
Livingstone College was founded in 1879 with entirely non-sectarian
academic programs. Today the college is a private, four-year,
coeducational institution which centers on the primary loyalties are first
in the church of Jesus Christ, while affirming that its purpose is to serve
the particular needs of the African Episcopal Zion Church and blacks
committed to the ministry of the church.

Location and Enrollment:

The 75 acre campus is located in Salisbury, North Carolina in an urban
environment. The city of Charlotte is 45 miles away from the college. The
campus has 22 buildings and a library which shelves over 69,000 volumes
of literature. Enrollment of the College is 750 students. With a
faculty-student ratio of 1-to-16.

Curriculum:

Livingstone's academic calendar is based on the semester system with
Baccalaureate degrees offered in the Bachelor of Arts, Bachelor of
Science, and Bachelor of Social Work. Undergraduate majors include:
Biology, Business and Commerce, Education, Music Liberal Arts,
Psychology, Physical Education, English and Literature, Foreign
Language, Mathematics, Music Therapy, Physical Sciences and Social
Sciences. Special programs offered are the Social Welfare Program,
and the Dual Degree Engineering Program.

Financial:

Tuition/fees per semester costs approximately $2,200; room and board
per semester is $1,700; annual fees are $400. Approximately 90 percent
of the students receive financial aid. Applications are based on need, as
well as, academic performance. The college participates in the following
programs: grants, loans, and employment.

University of Maryland Eastern Shore
Princess Anne, Maryland 21853
(410) 651-2200

History:

The University of Maryland Eastern Shore(UMES) had its origin on September 13, 1886. Initiated under the auspices of the Delaware Conference of the Methodist Episcopal Church, the Delaware Conference Academy was established in Princess Anne on that date with nine students and one faculty member. The State of Maryland assumed control of the Princess Anne Academy and renamed it the Eastern Shore Branch of the Maryland Agricultural College in 1919. In 1926, the College became the complete ownership of the state and University of Maryland was designated as the administrative agency. On July 1, 1970 the school became the University of Maryland Eastern Shore. UMES has developed an academic program that is perhaps more impressive than any other higher educational institution of its size in the East.

Location and Enrollment:

The UMES campus is located less than a half mile from the center of the small historical town of Princess Anne, fifteen minutes from the growing young town of Salisbury, 35 minutes from the exciting resort of Ocean City, and less than three hours from Baltimore City or Washington, D.C. The setting provides for serious academic study and an intimate atmosphere for learning. The University's current enrollment exceeds 2,500 students.

Curriculum:

The University offers a number of Undergraduate Degree programs: Bachelor of Science(B.S.), Bachelor of Arts(B.A.) and Teacher Education; Pre-Professional programs, UMES/UMAB Honors Program. Responsibility for knowing and meeting all degree requirements for graduation in any curriculum rest with the student. Total semester requirements total 41 hours. The cooperative education program is designed to enhance the departmental curriculum by integrating classroom theory with planned and supervised, full-time periods of practical work experience in a student's academic major.

Financial:

Several financial aid programs are offered. The average semester tuition for a non-boarding resident is $1,337 and $3,519 for a non-boarding, non-resident. Room and board is about $2,000 per semester.

Medgar-Evers College of the City University of New York
Brooklyn, New York 11225
(718) 270-4900 or (718) 270-6022

History:

Medgar-Evers College is one of the seventeen colleges which make up the City University of New York, the largest public municipal university of the world. The college was named in honor of Black civil rights leader, Medgar Evers, who was assassinated in 1963 in Mississippi.

Location and Enrollment:

Located in central Brooklyn, New York, Medgar-Evers College offers a wide variety of events as well as recreational activities to attend, such as the easy access to Coney Island Amusement Park, the Botanical Islands and Prospect Park. Medgar-Evers College is near the Brooklyn Bridge and easily accessible to public transportation, (such as busses and subway). The current enrollment at the college is nearly 5,000 full-time and part-time students.

Curriculum:

The degrees offered at the college are as follows: -Bachelor in Public Administration, Accounting, Early Childhood and Elementary Education, Nursing, Biology and Business Administration.

Financial:

Tuition cost is $1,050 per semester for in-state and $1,338 per semester for out-of-state students. Financial aid is awarded on the basis of need and academic performance at Medgar-Evers College. Every possible measure is taken to secure a quality education to furthering their education. Financial aid is available in all federal and state grants and loan programs. Scholarships are given and received from various sources. Employment is also available through the college work-study program.

Meharry Medical College
Nashville, Tennessee 37208
(615) 327-6000

History:

Meharry Medical College, founded in 1876, is perhaps the largest single educator of African-American health care professionals in the United States. Meharry's 26-acre campus houses a school of Medicine, Dentistry, Graduate studies, Allied Health Professions, Meharry/Hubbard Hospital and two health centers. Meharry offers an opportunity to low income and high risk students from social, economic or educational backgrounds which may otherwise rule out advanced professional training.

Location and Enrollment:

This private, one-to-five year graduate, co-educational college is located in the heart of Nashville, Tennessee. Nashville, a city of beautiful lakes and parks, houses over 500,000 residents. Meharry has a current enrollment of 900 students.

Curriculum:

Meharry has a regular academic program that offers a four-year curriculum in the basic and clinical sciences. Currently, 64 students are accepted into this program annually. The College has a special academic program that provides an enriched, five-year curriculum to students pursuing the M.D. Degree. The special medical student takes the regular nine month freshman curriculum over a period of fifteen months, starting in June of the summer prior to the beginning of the sophomore academic year. At that point, the student either transfers to the regular sophomore class or moves ahead with a decreased load taking two years to complete the sophomore year. Currently 16 students per year are accepted into this program. A limited number of the regular medical students are accepted into the M.D./P.H.D. program. This program, as well as the Medical Scholars Program at Meharry, requires that students demonstrate superior research potential prior to entering medical school and that students conduct a sophisticated laboratory research project in one or more of the basic science areas.

Financial:

Tuition is approximately $16,000 per year. Assistance is available through a number of programs (grants/loans). The Institution is a participant in the Health Profession Student Loan Program. The yearly cost at Meharry varies per school.

**Miles College
Birmingham, Alabama 35208
(205) 923-2771**

History:

Founded in 1905 by the Christian Methodist Episcopal Church, Miles College has had a mission to provide a program for its students which promotes the growth and development of young people who may have otherwise been denied an education.

Location and Enrollment:

Miles College is located in western Birmingham in the urban area of the city. The campus area is 35 acres with seventeen buildings including the college library which houses approximately 83,000 volumes of text for its student and faculty members. The residence halls at Miles College can house up to 300 students. Miles current enrollment exceeds 800 full-time students.

Curriculum:

The colleges academic calendar is based on the semester system with degrees offered in the following areas of study: Bachelor and Associate of Arts, Sciences: Top three majors include Business Administration, Communications and Social Sciences. Dual Degree programs and cooperative programs include Engineering, Veterinary Medicine and Allied Health.

Financial:

The cost of annual tuition at Miles College totals a sum of $3,800, including class and/or miscellaneous fees. Room and board averages a cost of $2,400 per year. There are approximately 95 percent of students which require some form of financial assistance in order to complete their education. Miles College participates in financial aid programs which will meet every students financial needs: Loans (NDSL and GSL/FISL), Grants (BEOG, SEOG and ASSIG), Scholarships and Employment.

Mississippi Valley State University
Itta Bena, Mississippi 38941
(601) 254-9041

History:

Mississippi Valley State University was created by an Act of the Mississippi State Legislature as Mississippi Vocational College in 1946. It was opened for service to students in the summer of 1950. In 1964, the Institution was renamed Mississippi Valley State College. Ten years later: 1974, the Legislature passed a bill elevating the young Institution to University status.

Location and Enrollment:

Mississippi Valley State University is located on a 450-acre tract adjacent to U.S. Highway 82, one mile from the town of Itta Bena, eight miles from the town of Greenwood, and 50 miles from the town of Greenville. There are 26 major buildings, plus 46 housing buildings for faculty and staff. The physical plant is valued at approximately twenty-five million dollars. The average enrollment is 2,200.

Curriculum:

MVSU awards the Bachelor of Arts, Bachelor of Science, Bachelor of Music, and the Master of Science in Environmental Health. The University has nine departments and 17 majors. Students may select majors in the following areas: Business Administration, Computer Science, Mathematics, Music Education, Elementary Education, Health Physical Education and Recreation, Industrial Technology, Social Work, Art, Speech, Biology, Environmental Health, Criminal Justice, Political Science, Office Administration, Sociology, and English.

Financial:

Tuition, room and board and fees for an average student are approximately $4,075 per year (in-state) and $6,000 (out-of-state), excluding books and supplies. The University has a program of financial assistance tailored to fit individual needs which includes Supplemental Educational Grants, National Direct Student Loans, Pell Grants, Federally Insured Loans, State Student Incentive Grants and Work Scholarships. Students may participate in the Cooperative Education Program. They are also eligible to compete for other institutional scholarships.

Morehouse College
Atlanta, Georgia 30314
(404) 681-2800 or (800) 851-1254

History:

Morehouse was originally founded as an all male institution in 1867. Now a private, coeducational four-year college, Morehouse is accredited by the Southern Association of Colleges and Schools. The newest edition to the college, the Morehouse School of Medicine, was established in 1975. The objective of the new edition was and is, to help create a larger pool of Black practicing physicians particularly for underserved minority communities.

Location and Enrollment:

Morehouse covers 40 acres of land in the beautiful city of Atlanta, capitol city of Georgia. The school has 25 buildings and the library houses nearly 240,000 volumes. Student population is approximately 2,900 with 112 full-time faculty members, 71 percent of whom hold doctorates. The faculty/student ratio is 16-to-1.

Curriculum:

Morehouse College's academic calendar is based on the semester system with Bachelor Degrees available in Bachelor of Arts and Bachelor of Science. The student has the opportunity to choose from over 20 undergraduate majors and the school also offers special programs which are the Study Abroad, Independent Study and the Honors program. Army, Navy and the Air Force offer ROTC programs.

Financial:

The cost of the semester tuition totals $3,325. Expected charges for room and board are $2,300 per semester. Financial aid is available and nearly 75 percent of the total student body receive some form of assistance by way of loans, grants, scholarship or work-study.

Morgan State University
Baltimore, Maryland 21239
(410) 319-3333

History:

Founded in 1867, many of the nation's foremost Doctors, Lawyers, Scientists, Judge elected officials, Business people and other professionals began their successful careers at Morgan State University. Morgan graduates are counted among the Vanguard of America's leaders. According to the U.S. Department of Education, Morgan ranks highly among schools whose graduates ultimately earn Ph.D.'s. Morgan's philosophy is to expose students to diverse races, cultures and beliefs.

Location and Enrollment:

Morgan is located in Baltimore, Maryland, the major port city on the Chesapeake Bay. Students have ready access to a dazzling array of educational, cultural and recreational activities. By attending Morgan, students find themselves living in one of the nations "ten best" future employment markets by way of increasing defense and service related jobs. The student-teacher ratio at Morgan is very favorable. Current student enrollment is 5,500.

Curriculum:

Morgan offers Bachelor Degrees in 45 different areas through the College of Arts and Sciences; School of Business and Management; School of Engineering and School of Education and Urban Studies. The center for career development makes available career counseling, planning and placement services to the student. A second degree award will be granted to a graduate of an accredited college or university who satisfactorily completes a minimum of 30 hours with the requirements of the major department.

Financial:

Tuition for state residents is $1,263 per semester; non-residents pay $2,531; room and board fees are $2,420 per semester. Financial aid is available to students who require additional funding in order to complete their education or to enroll for the first time. Morgan is one of the most affordable institutions in the state of Maryland, with a wide variety of financial programs available.

Morris Brown College
Atlanta, Georgia 30314
(404) 220-0270

History:

On October 15, 1885, under a charter granted by the State of Georgia, Morris Brown College opened with two teachers and 107 students. The College department was established in 1894 and graduated its first class in 1898. A Theological Department was established in 1894 for the training of ministers. Six years later, its name changed to Turner Theological Seminary in honor of the Senior Bishop of the African Methodist Episcopal Church. Although in 1929, the College restored its original name. The primary mission of Morris Brown College is to provide educational opportunities in a Christian environment that will enable its students to become fully functional people in society.

Location and Enrollment:

Morris Brown College is a part of the fastest growing international city in the nation, Atlanta, Georgia. This city with a population of over two million provides college students with abundant advantages that enhance the college experience. The College is a private, co-educational, four-year degree granting institution consisting of a faculty of 175 and a student body of over 2,000.

Curriculum:

Candidates for Bachelor of Arts or Bachelor of Science Degrees must complete 124 credit hours with an average grade of "C" or better. The curriculum is designed under two large divisions, lower and upper. The lower embraces all work within the first two years. In the Liberal Arts curriculum, one may specialize in one of the broader academic fields as a basis for later professional training for the Ministry, Social Work, Medicine, Business or other professions.

Financial:

Total yearly cost (boarding students) is $12,460. Non-boarding is $7,796. Federal financial aid is available on a needs basis. The Pell, Supplemental Educational Opportunity Grant and other forms of aid are also available by
applying Financial Aid.

Morris College
Sumter, South Carolina 29150
(803) 775-9371

History:

Morris College was founded in 1908 originally as an elementary High School and College for the purpose of training "Negro Youth". The use of the word "Negro" was depleted from the charter in 1925, and the college began admitting all ethnic groups. The College is owned by the Baptist Education and Missionary Convention of South Carolina.

Location and Enrollment:

The College is located in Sumter, South Carolina with a 44-acre campus housing 15 buildings, including a relatively new library stocked with over 125,000 volumes of text. The current enrollment at the college totals 700 to 800 students.

Curriculum:

The College terms are based on the semester system with degrees offered as follows: Bachelor of Science in Education, Bachelor of Arts, Bachelor of Fine Arts Business Administration, Fine Arts, History, Social Studies, English, Elementary Education, Biology, Mathematics, Religious Education, Political Sciences, Business Education, Early Childhood Education, Technical Studies, Sociology, School Health Sciences, Community Health, Secondary Education and School Administration.

Financial:

Annual tuition, fees, room and board at Morris College is estimated at $7,000. Cost for non-boarding is $4,520. The students at Morris College requiring financial assistance may apply for financial aid depending on need and academic performance. The College participates in a variety of programs involved with funding for education.

Norfolk State University
Norfolk, Virginia 23504
(804) 683-8600

History:

Although first known in 1935 as the Junior College unit of Virginia Union University, success and expansion prevailed and in 1944, "was born Norfolk Division of Virginia State College." Nicknamed "Little State," this College had huge accomplishments in academics, sports, and community involvement. On February 1, 1969 by legislative enactment, Norfolk State College emerged. The belief that meeting education and professional needs of students through excellence in teaching, research and leadership in community service, Norfolk State University has succeeded in becoming a major urban university.

Location and Enrollment:

The 122-acre campus is located in urban Norfolk within two miles of downtown. Norfolk is surrounded on three sides by the sea. The city is less than a day's drive from the major metropolitan areas on the east coast. Public beaches, city lakes, bike trails and other recreational facilities, label Norfolk as "College Life." The University offers English as a foreign language and therefore has a wide variety of cultural backgrounds. The multi-ethnic student body is composed of 7,500 students from all sections of the United States and 35 foreign countries.

Curriculum:

General requirements for graduate study programs are established by the University. In general, applicants must hold a Baccalaureate Degree from an accredited institution and hold a 2.5 grade point average on a 4.0 scale. The University is organized into the following schools: Arts and Letters, Business, Health Related Professions and Natural Sciences, Education, Social Sciences, Social Work, Technology and Graduate Studies. There are more than 70 programs on the undergraduate level. Fifteen programs are offered for the graduate program.

Financial:

The estimated yearly tuition cost for a Virginia resident living off campus is $2,745 and on campus is $6,345. Non-residents pay $6,225 off campus and $9,625 on campus.

North Carolina A&T State University
Greensboro, North Carolina 27411
(919) 334-7500

History:

North Carolina Agricultural and Technical State University was founded in 1891 and is now affiliated with the University of North Carolina. The University is a four-year, coeducational, public institutional facility.

Location and Enrollment:

The University campus expands to 181 acres in urban Greensboro, North Carolina. There are more than 50 major structures on campus, including a multi-story library containing over 307,000 volumes and 1,500 periodicals.

The enrollment of the University is over 7,000 with 342 full-time faculty members, most of whom have earned a Ph.D.

Curriculum:

The University offers several Undergraduate and Graduate Degree Programs including Agriculture, Engineering, Chemistry, Biology, Nutrition/Dietitians, Reading, Elementary and Secondary Education and Guidance. In addition, A&T's Computer Research Department recently designed two computer chips which are currently being marketed. Degrees are offered in 25 programs. Military Science Programs with Air Force ROTC, Army Flight Training and Army ROTC are also offered.

Financial:

North Carolina A&T University participates in all financial aid programs, federal and state. The approximate cost of tuition per semester for in-state students is $684(off-campus) and $2,248(on-campus). Non-residents pay $3,716(off-campus) and $5,281(on-campus) per semester. The following are some of the programs in which the University participates: loans, grants, scholarships and employment.

North Carolina Central University
Durham, North Carolina 27707
(919) 560-6100

History:

North Carolina Central University was founded in 1910 and is a state-supported liberal arts institution. The basis of the college throughout its history has been to provide perspective and intellectual strength for the endeavors of a lifetime; and provision of a climate for high quality learning with social emphasis on education for intelligent, responsive participation in the home, the community, and a career.

Location and Enrollment:

The 101-acre campus and its 60 buildings are located in Durham, North Carolina, in the urban district of the community. The campus also includes a 400,000 volume library with 2,200 periodicals. The population of the college exceeds 6,000 students.

Curriculum:

There are over 25 Baccalaureate Degrees offered at North Carolina Central University and over 18 Graduate Degrees are offered in various subjects. Such as Mathematics, Chemistry, Biology, Psychology, Home Economics, Business and School Administration. North Carolina Central also has an accredited three-year law school.

Financial:

Approximate cost of tuition/fees plus room and board total $4,300 per year for residents and the cost for non-residents is $10,100. Financial aid is accepted and offered to over 85 percent of the students at the University. The programs offered include the following: loans (as needed), grants (state and federal), scholarships based upon academic achievement and employment.

Oakwood College
Huntsville, Alabama 35896
(205) 726-7000

History:

Oakwood College is owned by the Seventh-Day Adventists Church and was formed in 1896. The college has built its offerings around the philosophy that "true education" means more than the pursuance of a certain course of study. It means more than the preparation for the life that now is. It deals with the whole being...the harmonious development of the physical, the mental and the spiritual powers. It prepares the student for the joy of service in this world, and for the higher joy of wider service in the world to come.

Location and Enrollment:

The campus of Oakwood College is 980 acres situated in suburban Huntsville with the urban center located just one mile away. The institution consists of 17 buildings with a library containing approximately 80,000 volumes. The current enrollment at Oakwood College is approximately 1,300 with 69 full-time faculty members, 35 of which have earned Ph.D. degrees. The faculty-student ratio is 1-20.

Curriculum:

The College's academic calendar is based on the quarter system with Bachelor Degrees offered in over 26 different majors. Undergraduate majors may also be chosen from a wide variety of programs as well as special programs. Among the courses offered include Accounting, Communications, Computer Science, Engineering, Medical Technology and Premedicine.

Financial:

The approximate annual cost of study at Oakwood College is $6,384 for students living off-campus and $10,230 for on-campus students. Financial aid is available to students meeting the various financial aid requirements stated on applications. Oakwood College offers the following financial aid programs. loans, grants, scholarships and employment.

Paine College
Augusta, Georgia 30901
(404) 821-8200 or (800) 476-7703

History:

In 1882, each Church appointed three of its members to a committee
which established Paine Institute, named in honor of Bishop Robert
Paine. Six months after incorporation, classes began in rented quarters
on Broad Street in Augusta, Georgia. The present campus site on
Fifteenth Street was acquired in 1886. Throughout the years of its
history, Paine has been a distinctively Christian college. It has maintained
deep concern for the quest for truth, and has been resolute in blending
knowledge with values and personal commitment. Paine has been
historically dedicated to the preparation of holistic persons for responsible
life in society.

Location and Enrollment:

Paine College has a 50-acre campus located in the heart of Augusta,
Georgia. All the physical facilities of the College are located within a
geographical area bound by Fifteenth Street, Laney-Walker Boulevard,
Beman Street, and Central Avenue. Most of the College buildings,
including residence halls, classroom buildings and the library, are located
in the main campus area. Directly across the street from this area are the
athletic field, gymnasium and the chapel/music building. Current
enrollment is approximately 600.

Curriculum:

The curriculum of the College is designed to provide a balanced program
of its offerings in the areas of language, literature and fine arts; natural
sciences and mathematics; social sciences; religion and philosophy;
early childhood and middle grades education; and areas of concentration
on the secondary level in biology, business administration, chemistry,
English, history, mathematics, music, and sociology. The College
engages in continuous evaluation of its total program. 124 hours of
college work are required for a degree.

Financial:

Paine College offers grants, loans and part-time employment to assist
eligible students in meeting their educational expenses. Combined
Tuition, room and board for Paine College is approximately $4,500 for
students living on campus and $2,963 for students living off campus.

Paul Quinn College
Dallas, Texas 75241
(214) 376-1000

History:

Paul-Quinn College, which was founded in 1872, is a four-year, liberal arts college sponsored by the African Methodist Episcopal Church. The purpose of the college is to guide its students in the development of a wholesome Christian philosophy of life, to develop their ability to think and express themselves intelligently and objectively in a democracy and to build a sense of responsibility for the common good of our society.

Location and Enrollment:

The 22-acre campus of Paul Quinn College is now located in Dallas, Texas.The enrollment at the college is about 1,200 students with 40 full-time faculty members. The faculty-student ratio is 1-13.

Curriculum:

A wide variety of courses and degree programs make Paul Quinn College a fulfilling experience. The educational program is organized into four academic divisions and the Learning Resource Center. These include the Division of Arts and Sciences, Division of Professional Studies, Division of Education and the Division of Developmental Studies. The Learning Resource Center includes Library, Media and Technical Resources. A parallel-degree program with Texas State Technical Institute (TSTI) makes it possible for students to earn an Associate Degree from TSTI and a Bachelor of Applied Science Degree from Paul Quinn College. Nine such specialized programs are available.

Financial:

To assist in meeting educational expenses, Paul Quinn College offers a variety of financial aid programs, which include scholarships, loans, grants and work study programs. Ninety-eight percent of the student population at Paul-Quinn College receive some type of financial assistance. The cost per semester for tuition fees, and room and board total $3,500.

Philander-Smith College
Little Rock, Arkansas 72202
(501) 373-9845

History:

Philander-Smith College is known historically to be the first institution to offer the Bachelor Degree to African-Americans and also, the first college of higher education in Arkansas to produce college graduates for leadership in public schools, church, industry, and government. The only four-year college open to African-Americans for over 70 years in Little Rock, Philander-Smith graduates over 50% of all African-American physicians practicing in the area. The college was founded in 1877 and chartered in 1883 with a continuing mission to provide a quality education to all.

Location and Enrollment:

Philander-Smith College campus is located in Little Rock, Arkansas. The campus size is 24 acres with 12 buildings and a 60,000 volume library. The current enrollment at the College is 1,000.

Curriculum:

The College calendar is based on the semester system with Baccalaureate Degrees offered in over 21 major subjects, including Biology, Geology, Nutrition/Dietetics and Psychology. Majors are available to the student body under various programs with other special programs being also available.

Financial:

Tuition for on-campus students per semester is $2,687, and students living off campus is $1,450; room and board is $1,238. Approximately 85 percent of the student body at Philander-Smith College receives some form of financial assistance. The college offers the following financial aid programs: loans, grants, scholarships and on-campus employment.

Prairie View A&M University
Prairie View, Texas 77446
(409) 857-3311

History:

Prairie View Agricultural and Mechanical University was founded in 1876 as a state-supported liberal arts institution on a professional land-grant. The Institution is accredited by the Southern Association of Colleges and Schools, Texas Education Agency and the Association of Texas Colleges and Universities. The University is a member of the Texas A&M University System.

Location and Enrollment:

The Institution is located in Waller County, Prairie View, Texas, which is located 46 miles northwest of Houston, Texas. The campus consists of 1,440 acres located in the suburbs. The University has 65 buildings and a 400,000 volume library. The student enrollment at the college is over 5,000.

Curriculum:

Prairie View offers a wide variety of Undergraduate, and Graduate Degree programs in subjects such as Finance, Economics, Engineering, Accounting, Marketing, School Administration, and Guidance. There are also special Science, Reading, Business and Music Education courses available.. Other special programs are also offered. The University also offers Army ROTC, Navy ROTC, and Navy Flight Training.

Financial:

There are approximately 80 percent of students at Prairie View who receive some form of financial aid. The approximate cost of tuition, fees and room and board for in-state students is $2,572 per semester and for out-of-state students, $4,611. Out-of-state students can compete for in-state scholarships. Prairie View participates in loans, grants, scholarships and on-campus employment.

Rust College
Holly Springs, Mississippi 38635
(601) 252-4661

History:

Rust College was founded by the Freedman's Aid Society of the Methodist Episcopal Church, in 1866. At that time, Mississippi and the south were devastated by four-years of war, groups such as Freedman's Aid Society provided education for thousands of newly freed slaves. Of the 4,000 such schools which came into being the majority failed to survive more than a few years. Rust College, however, did survive and is flourishing today. It is the oldest historically black college in the state, as well as Mississippi's second oldest college. Rust succeeded to train former slaves to become teachers and preachers and worthy members of their communities.

Location and Enrollment:

The College is located in the city of Holly Springs in northwest Mississippi. Situated approximately 35 miles southeast of Memphis, Tennessee. The College is on U.S. highway 78 and Mississippi highway 17, and is easily accessible from Mississippi highway 4. Two bus lines pass through the city. The current enrollment at Rust is 1,000 students, 90 percent of which live on campus.

Curriculum:

The curriculum at Rust College is derived from broad disciplines as well as the specialized subjects falling within these broad areas. The curriculum is under constant study and revision in response to changing society and growing complexity of problems. Course offerings are organized under five divisions, a sixth division, freshman studies which is an inter-disciplinary program designed to aid the student in acclimating himself to college work. The divisions are as follows: Division of Business, Social Science, Education, Humanities, Science and Mathematics.

Financial:

A full-time student's schedule of expenses per year is approximately $6,600. Rust College will not deny an education to any qualified applicant simply on the basis of his/her inability to pay. Federal State Grants-in-Aid and the United Methodist Grant help ease the burden of paying for a college education. There are also scholarships, loans, grants and work-study programs available.

Saint Augustine's College
Raleigh, North Carolina 27610-2298
(919) 516-4000

History:

Saint Augustine's College was founded in 1867 by the Protestant
Episcopal Church. Today it is a private, four-year, coeducational college
accredited by the Southern Association of Colleges and Schools.

Location and Enrollment:

The College is located on a 130-acre campus in the urban center of
Raleigh. Forty-three buildings comprise the institution's facilities. The
current enrollment at the College is close to 2,000.

Curriculum:

The College's academic calendar is based on the semester system.
Degrees offered include the Bachelor of Arts and the Bachelor of
Science. Undergraduate majors are offered in over 10 fields of study
including Journalism, Marketing, Management, Economics, Accounting,
Engineering, Chemistry and Physics. Special programs offered are the
Cooperative Education, Study Abroad, Independent Study and the
Honors Program. Other special programs include Freshman Studies
Program and Special Services Program. Cooperative Education is also
available.

Financial:

Current estimated cost at Saint Augustine's College for boarding students
is $9,773 per year and $6,175 for non-boarding students. Saint
Augustine's goal is to provide a financial aid package to cover the
difference between the student's budget and the amount revealed by his
or her official needs analysis. The Business Office will make reasonable
payment agreements to cover that difference, if any.

Saint Paul's College
Lawrenceville, Virginia 23868
(804) 848-3111

History:

Small in number, as compared to the humanity they serve, are the salient figures of history. One such figure was James Solomon Russell, founder and first Principal of Saint Paul's College. On September 24, 1888, with fewer than a dozen students, Saint Paul's College was started in the building known as the Saul Building. More students came, as word about the school traveled. The members increased to such an extent that the Reverend Russell realized the need for a program of expansion and development. The history of Saint Paul's College and its development are reflected in the basic aims and the philosophy of the College as it stands today. The achievements of its graduates, throughout the world, give evidence of the zeal, sacrifice, and educational foresight which have characterized its workers and leaders throughout the years.

Location and Enrollment:

Saint Paul's College is a 75-acre campus located in Lawrenceville, Virginia. It is easily accessible by I-85 and Highway 46. To assure personal counseling and intellectual growth, Saint Paul's College limits its total enrollment to not more than 720. Thus, their student-teacher ratio remains 17-1.

Curriculum:

Saint Paul's College offers the Bachelor of Science Degree in over 10 areas of study, and the Bachelor of Arts Degree in 3 areas. Majors include Sociology, Political Science, Business Administration, Biology, Mathematics, Environmental Science and English. St. Paul's also offers a Single-Parent Support System which provides a living/learning environment for single parents with children. The parents attend classes eleven months of the year and may complete an undergraduate degree program in three years.

Financial:

The estimated total cost for one school year at Saint Paul's is $9,100 for boarding students, and $5,200 for non-boarding students. The College offers grants, loans, scholarships and employment to assist students with their educational expenses.

Savannah State College
Savannah, Georgia 31404
(912) 356-2186

History:

By Act of the General Assembly on November 26, 1890, the State of
Georgia "established in connection with the State University, and forming
one of the departments thereof, a school for the education and training of
Negro students." In September 1979, the faculty and students in the
Division of Education at Savannah State College were transferred to
Armstrong State College and Savannah State College received the
faculty and students in the Division of Business from Armstrong State
College in a historic program swap. This resulted in the creation of a new
School of Business during the 1979-80 academic year.

Location and Enrollment:

The college is located in Thunderbolt, Georgia just outside of the city
limits of Savannah. Current enrollment is close to 3,000 students.

Curriculum:

All Bachelor's Degree programs and associate degree programs require
that students complete a 90 quarter credit hour core of general education
courses. Savannah State College comprises three schools: Business;
Humanities and Social Sciences; and Sciences and Technology.
Through its three schools, the College awards the baccalaureate degree,
with majors in Accounting, Information Systems Management,
Marketing, English Language and Literature, Music, Criminal Justice,
History, Political Science, Social Work, Sociology, Chemistry, Biology,
Marine Biology, Environmental Studies, Mathematics, Civil Engineering
Technology, Mechanical Engineering Technology, Electronic Engineering
Technology, Process Engineering Technology, Mass Communications,
Computer Science Technology, and Physics. An Associate of Science
degree is offered with majors in Marine Science Technology, Chemical
Engineering Technology, and Computer Technology. Additionally,
Savannah State College offers an Associate of Science degree in a dual
arrangement with the Savannah Area Vocational-Technical School in the
areas of Chemical, Civil, Design and Drafting, Electronic and Mechanical
Technology.

Financial:

Tuition for in-state students living on campus is $1,350, off campus
$580. Tuition for out-of-state students living on campus is $2,271, off
campus $1,501.

Selma University
Selma, Alabama 36701
(205) 872-2533

History:

Selma University was founded in 1878 in affiliation with the Baptist Church. The University is accredited by the State of Alabama. Selma University is a public, four-year, coeducational College.

Location and Enrollment:

The University is located in the city of Selma, Alabama in an urban setting. The campus is 35-acres with 12 buildings, a library, and residence halls which can accommodate 350 students. The current enrollment is approximately 600 students.

Curriculum:

The academic calendar at Selma University is based on the semester system. Degree's offered include: Associate in Arts, Associate in Science and Bachelor of Theology. Undergraduate majors include Liberal Arts, Business, General Education, Pre-nursing, Pre-medical and computer science. Special programs include Upper Bound and Honor Societies.

Financial:

Cost per semester is $2,300 for tuition and fees and $1,850 for room and board. Ninety-eight percent of the student body receives some form of financial aid. Selma University offers programs such as: loans, grants, and employment.

Shaw University
Raleigh, North Carolina 27601
(919) 546-8200

History:

Founded in 1865 by Henry Martin Tupper to teach Freedman Theology and Biblical Interpretation, the institution was known as the Raleigh Institute. In 1870 it became Shaw Collegiate Institute and eventually changed to Shaw University in 1875. Coeducational from its very inception, Shaw recognizes the equality of all races and sexes. Indeed, its mission as a church-related institution involves providing educational opportunities for students from all social-economic groups. Today, after 122 years of existence, Shaw University continues to build on its liberal arts tradition, a tradition that espouses learning in the humanities, social and natural sciences, and the quantitative disciplines.

Location and Enrollment:

Shaw University is located in the city of Raleigh, North Carolina. Raleigh Memorial Auditorium is across the street from Shaw University and offers various events. There are theaters and a mall near the University as well as a civic center with numerous programs to attend. Current enrollment is 2,300.

Curriculum:

Shaw University is a liberal arts, vocational-oriented institution committed to training today's youth for the world of work and service. The University is committed to the training of persons who are interested in being teachers, lawyers, doctors, dentists and the like. This instruction is provided in Teacher Education, Pre-Professional Studies, Pre-Engineering, Pre-Theology, and other areas to which a liberal arts education is pertinent. Divisions of Human Resources, Human Development, Business and Public Administration are the major fields of study offered.

Financial:

Financial aid at Shaw University consists of scholarships, grants, loans and jobs awarded singly or in the form of a "package" to meet a student's financial need. Total cost per year for an on-campus student is $8,936, an off-campus student pays $5,562.

Shorter College
North Little Rock, Arkansas 72114
(501) 374-6305

History:

Founded in 1886, Shorter College believes that every human being should have the opportunity to develop his or her innate abilities and talents to their maximum potentials. Shorter College also believes that the development and welfare of a society are contingent upon the educational opportunities which a society offers its citizenry. Shorter College, a small, private, coeducational, two-year junior college in North Little Rock, Arkansas is one of eight institutions of higher learning in the United States that are affiliated with the African Methodist Episcopal Church. Shorter is predominately black; but the college seeks to provide educational opportunities for persons of all races. It is interracial, as well as nonsectarian in admissions.

Location and Enrollment:

The College is located in the small, quiet city of North Little Rock off Interstate 40. The small town is personable and a small college offers more opportunities to be successful not only in the classroom, but in a number of areas. Most class sizes are 20 or less, meaning that instructors will get to know and analyze academic abilities of every student. The current enrollment is approximately 250.

Curriculum:

Liberal Arts programs are available for an Associate Degree and for junior year entry at four-year colleges. Fields of study include; Business Administration, Secretarial Science, Foundations for Education, Foundations for Social Work, Fire Science, Social Science and Liberal Arts.

Financial:

Tuition is $89 per credit hour; room and board totals $1,200 per semester. Some students find that special help is needed in overcoming educational cost. Shorter College not only concerns itself with individualized instruction, tutorial service and programs to enhance basis skills through development of education through financial aid packages and student assistance in applying for aid. Tuition, room and board at Shorter College is considerably lower than the national average for private colleges. Shorter participates in grants, loans, scholarship and/or employment programs.

Simmon's Bible College
Louisville, Kentucky 40210
(502) 776-1443

History:

Simmon's Bible College was founded in 1873 by the General Association of Baptist in Kentucky. Simmon's long-living mission has been to instill a comprehensive bible knowledge in the students which turn to the college for guidance and a better understanding of the Christian doctrine.

Location and Enrollment:

Simmon's Bible College is located in Louisville, Kentucky. Louisville is easily reached by way of Interstate 71 South from eastern/northern United States and 71 North from western United States. Louisville is centered between Owensboro and Lexington with the Ohio river approximately an hour drive away. The current student enrollment at the college is 150.

Curriculum:

Baccalaureate Degrees are available to students in the following areas: -Biblical Literature, -Religious Education and -Theology. The college instructor's teach from the perspective of the biblical ethnic as found in the Old and New Testaments, as well as, personal background and experience in today's society.

Financial:

The college accepts and works with students in obtaining necessary financial assistance in order to finance their education. Financial aid is available to students in the form of grants, loans, employment, and/or scholarships based on need and academic performance. Applications are processed on the areas of need and academic potential. Tuition fees are $20 per credit hour. Registration fee is $20.

Sojourner-Douglass College
Baltimore, Maryland 21205
(410) 276-0306

History:

Sojourner-Douglass College was opened in 1972, created as the Homestead-Montebello Center of Antioch University. The College name was derived in honor of the historical contributions of two Black Americans-Sojourner Truth and Frederick Douglass. The college was opened as a means to educate adult learners who have been by-passed. The mission of the college is to increase students abilities for self-expression, self-development and engagement in effective social action as members of a world community.

Location and Enrollment:

Sojourner-Douglass College is located in the heart of Baltimore in Maryland. The primary administrative and classroom facilities are housed in the Dunbar Community School Complex, which is a multi-purpose, multi-educational complex. The current full-time enrollment figure at the college stands at nearly 500.

Curriculum:

The College is a four-year, independent institution which offers Bachelor of Arts Degrees in applied and social sciences, which is covered in the following: Psychology/Counseling, Social Work, Social Welfare, Criminal Justice, Community-Urban Development, Management and Administration, Early Childhood Education, Human Growth and Development, Human and Social Resources.

Financial:

The College distributes financial aid on demonstrated need. Applications are available to all students. The school calendar is based on trimester; tuition for one class is $591, two classes $1,100, and a full (12 credit) load of 4 or more classes is $1,700. The school participates in the following programs of financial assistance: GSL (student must maintain a 2.0 average or higher), Pell Grant, Maryland State Scholarship and Scholarships accepted from personal student research.

South Carolina State University
Orangeburg, South Carolina 29117
(803) 536-7000

History:

Founded in 1896, for almost a century, young people have come to South Carolina State College in search of opportunities to enhance their lives. Thousands have found a key to a bright, successful future. South Carolina is a historically black college which carries students from small towns, big cities, other states, and foreign countries.

Location and Enrollment:

The campus is 147-acres with 60 buildings and 12 dormitories located very close to the center of South Carolina. Orangeburg is an ideal location for college. Easy to get to from any direction, a five minute walk from downtown's restaurants, and a modern mall with over 30 shops. Three other colleges are nearby expanding social possibilities. Enrollment consists of over 5,000 men and women of which 58 percent live on campus.

Curriculum:

South Carolina State offers more than 60 major fields of study. A total of between 120 and 137 semester hours is required for graduation. The University offers both Bachelor of Arts and Bachelor of Science Degrees. There are hundreds of courses within the major or minor fields including Agribusiness, Biology, Chemistry, General Science, Mathematics, Nutrition, Home Economics, Speech, Early Childhood Education, Special Nursing, Technical Education and Music Merchandising offered, covering subjects from the most traditional, to the most modern.

Financial:

South Carolina residents deciding to live on campus can expect to pay $2,743 a semester. Out-of-state students pay $3,983. There are grants, loans, student work aid and scholarships to help cover these costs.

Southern University
Baton Rouge, LA 70813-2020
(504) 771-5115

History:

Southern University was chartered by the Louisiana General Assembly in 1880 in New Orleans. In 1914 the University was relocated in Baton Rouge on property locally referred to as Scott's Bluff. From three buildings, twelve students and five faculty members, the University has experienced phenomenal growth since those early years.

Location and Enrollment:

The University is located in the capital city of Louisiana. Baton Rouge is approximately 90 miles to the west of New Orleans, also known as the Crescent City. The population of Baton Rouge is rapidly approaching the 400,000 mark. The climate is temperate with temperatures reaching 90 degrees or more during summer months and rarely falling below freezing during winter months. The University has over 10,000 students from 49 states and 44 countries.

Curriculum:

Bachelors degrees are offered through the colleges of: Agriculture and Home Economics, Arts and Humanities, Business, Education, Engineering, Sciences, The School of Nursing, the School of Public Policy and Urban Affairs and the School of Architecture. Masters Degrees offered through the colleges of: Arts and Humanities, Education, Sciences, The School of Accountancy and the School of Public Policy and Urban Affairs. Doctoral and Professional Degrees offered through: The College of Education, The Southern University Law Center, The School of Public Policy and Urban Affairs, The School of Accountancy and The School of Nursing. Associate Degrees are offered through the college of: Engineering and Sciences.

Financial:

Per semester tuition, room and board for in-state students is $1,975, out-of-state students pay $3,288. Southern University offers an extensive financial aid program -- including University-sponsored scholarships, Pell Grant, Supplemental Educational Opportunity Grant, student loans, college work study, and many state sponsored aid programs. Apply for financial aid as soon as possible after January 1 of your senior year.

**Southern University
New Orleans, Louisiana 70126
504) 286-5000**

History:

Founded in 1959, Southern University is a public, four-year coeducational institution which has had a mission since its establishment to provide a quality education to people who wished advancement.

Location and Enrollment:

Southern University has a 22-acre campus and is located in the city of New Orleans. Readily available is easy access of public transportation. The current full-time student enrollment at the Institution is approximately 5,000. The faculty-student ratio is 1 to 30.

Curriculum:

The academic calendar at Southern University is based on the semester system. Degrees offered include the Bachelor of Arts, Bachelor of Science, Associate of Arts. There are over 20 undergraduate majors including Journalism, Modern Languages, Office Administration, Secretarial Science, Technical Education, Economics, Business Administration and Criminal Justice.

Financial:

Tuition costs for residents is $828 per semester; non-residents is $1,713. Tuition and fees are based on the students city of residency. Approximately 90 percent of the student population receives some form of financial aid including: loans, grants, scholarship and employment in order to fund their education.

Southern University
Shreveport, Louisiana 71107
(318) 674-3300

History:

This extension of the Southern University system was founded in 1964
as a two-year, co-educational, commuter community college. As an
integral part of the University's triad, the Shreveport institution shares
the same mission -- to provide a quality education to people who wish
to advance.

Location and Enrollment:

The 101-acre suburban campus is located in Shreveport-Bossier City.
Total enrollment is under 1,000 students.

Curriculum:

The academic calendar at this two-year extension of Southern University
is based on the semester system. Associate Degrees are offered in
Accounting, Banking and Finance, Biology, Business Administration,
Chemistry, Computer Sciences, Electronic Technology, Hotel/Motel and
Restaurant Management, Legal Assistant/Paralegal, Marketing and
Distribution, Mathematics, Medical Assistant, Medical Laboratory/
Technologies, Medical Records Technology, Mental Health/Human
Services, Pre-elementary Education, Respiratory Therapy Technology,
Science Technologies, Secretarial and Related Programs, Small Business
Management and Ownership, Social Sciences, Surgical Technology,
Teacher Aide and Word Processing.

Financial:

Tuition for residents is approximately $828 per semester; non-residents is
$1,713. Tuition and Fees are based on the student's city of residency. Pell
grants, minority scholarships, loans and jobs are available for students
needing financial aid.

Southwestern Christian College
Terrell, Texas 75160
(214) 524-3341

History:

Southwestern Christian College has had a mission for 50 years to educate its students to their fullest potential and for students to learn to live a productive life with respect to themselves and others. The Institution today is a private, two-year, coeducational college.

Location and Enrollment:

The campus at Southwestern Christian College is 25 acres situated in rural Terrell, Texas. Dallas, the capital city of Texas, is located just 33 miles from the college campus. Fifteen buildings and a library are on the campus grounds with a library that houses over 30,000 volumes of text. The current enrollment at the college is over 300 with 19 full-time faculty members.

Curriculum:

The College's academic calendar is based on the semester system. Degrees offered include the Associate of Arts and the Associate of Science. Undergraduate majors include: science, English, Biology, Business, Religion, Music, Speech, Secretarial Science, Home Economics, Social Science, History, Psychology, Mathematics and Physical Education. Special programs offered are the adult evening classes which include vocational areas.

Financial:

Cost at the college per semester for tuition, fees and room/board is approximately $2,078. The cost of room and board is $1,511. Financial aid is available by means of grants, loans, employment, NDSL, Texas Equalization Grants and Work-Study grants. There are over 95 percent of students at the college which receive some type of financial assistance.

Spelman College
Atlanta, Georgia 30314
(404) 681-3643

History:

Spelman's history dates from 1881, when two remarkable women opened a school in the basement of Atlanta's Friendship Baptist Church. The pupils were mostly women out of slavery, determined to learn to read the Bible and write well enough to send letters to their families in the North. With a proud sense of dedication and commitment, Sophia Packard and Harriet Giles functioned as a close and effective partnership to lay the foundation for this magnificent institution. By the time Spelman had celebrated its 25th anniversary, the Institution had filled a whole spectrum of needs for thousands of black women -- from grade school through trade school and college.

Location and Enrollment:

The 32-acre campus is situated in the urban center of Atlanta. This private, women's liberal arts college has a total full-time enrollment of approximately 2,000 students.

Curriculum:

As an outstanding historically black college for women, Spelman strives for academic excellence in liberal education. Degrees offered include the Bachelor Arts and the Bachelor of Science. The College provides students with an academic climate conducive to the full development of their intellectual and leadership potential. The College is a member of the Atlanta University Center Consortium. Spelman students enjoy the benefits of a small college, while having access to the resources of the other five participating institutions.
The educational program is designed to give students a comprehensive liberal arts background through study in the fine arts, humanities, social sciences and natural sciences. The college's academic calendar is based on the semester system.

Financial:

Basic annual cost for tuition, fees, room and board is approximately $13,042 for students living on campus and $7,792 for students living off campus. This does not include amounts for books, supplies and travel expenses. Spelman College offers the following financial aid programs: loans, grants, and employment.

**Stillman College
Tuscaloosa, Alabama 35403
(205) 349-4240**

History:

Stillman College, founded in 1876 by the Presbyterian Church, U.S., is a four year, liberal arts college offering the Bachelor of Arts and Bachelor of Science degrees. The College bears the name of Dr. Charles Allen Stillman who came to Tuscaloosa in 1870 as pastor of the First Presbyterian Church. The aim of the College is to prepare students for places of leadership and service in society, and for lives which have Christian value and meaning.

Location and Enrollment:

Stillman is located in Tuscaloosa, Alabama which is 52 miles southwest of Birmingham and 90 miles northeast of Meridian, Mississippi. The 100-acre campus is within walking distance of downtown Tuscaloosa. The enrollment at Stillman College is nearly 800 students, with a staff of 52 full-time faculty members. The faculty-student ratio is 1-to-15.

Curriculum:

The curriculum at the College is offered on the semester system and Baccalaureate Degrees are offered as follows: Biology, Business, Chemistry, Communications, Computer Science, Elementary Education, English, Health and Physical Education, History, Mathematics, Music, Physics, Sociology, , Religion and Philosophy. Special programs offered are Cooperative Education, Liberal Arts and Engineering combinations and the Honors Program.

Financial:

Cost to live on campus per semester is approximately $4,460. Off campus per semester is $2,230. Approximately 90 percent of the total student body at the College receive some form of financial assistance. Therefore, the college participates in all financial aid programs.

Talladega College
Talladega, Alabama 35160
(205) 362-0206

History:

In the fall of 1851, the Coosa River Baptist Association, meeting in Calhoun County, resolved to erect a "Baptist Male High School" in Talladega. The school which was originally named after General Wagner B. Swayne was changed to Talladega College in 1867. According to Fountain Gage Ragland, who came as a student in 1868, it was "the first such building for Negroes thousands had ever seen.

Location and Enrollment:

Talladega College strives to create an environment which focuses on the intellectual, social, spiritual and physical growth and development of each student. Students are encouraged to become active participants in their own development and to take advantage of the total educational experience offered by the College. Student population averages 900.

Curriculum:

The Institution offers a variety of Undergraduate majors in the Humanities, Natural Sciences and Social Sciences. Undergraduate degrees are offered in Physical Therapy, Nursing, Health Science, Engineering, Economics, Computer Science, Chemistry, Biology, Public Administration, Social Work, Psychology, Sociology, Rehabilitation, Education and Business Administration are available in Physical Therapy, Nursing and Health Sciences.

Financial:

Combined tuition, fees, room and board at Talladega is $8,240. Awards are based upon academic merit and financial need. The maximum amount of any award cannot exceed the student's need as determined by CSS and Talladega College. Four kinds of financial assistance are available: scholarships, grants, part time employment, and loans. Students seeking financial assistance should file their application with the director of financial aid. All financial help is made available in two equal installments during the academic year.

Tennessee State University
Nashville, Tennessee 37203
(615) 320-3131

History:

Although founded in 1912, the Institute as it exists today is the result of a
1979 merger of Tennessee State University and the University of
Tennessee at Nashville (established in 1971).

Location and Enrollment:

As the city's only public, four-year institution, Tennessee State University
has a Main Campus located in a residential area of Nashville, and a
Downtown Campus is located in the heart of the city. The more than 7,500
students enrolled at both campuses have a variety of cultural backgrounds.

Curriculum:

The University's academic calendar is based on the semester system
and offers programs which meet the needs of day and evening students.
All entering freshmen are admitted to the University College. This
program allows a systematic progression through the core curriculum
required in all degree programs. The University College provides a
mechanism for students to improve academic skills and explore career
options before declaring a major. Students must complete 37 credit
hours and maintain a minimum 2.0 grade point average (GPA) in the
University College before they are admitted to a degree-granting school.
Once students declare majors, they pursue upper-level courses
preparing them for employment or additional study at graduate or
professional schools. Undergraduate degrees offer a number of options
for majors such as: Architectural Engineering, Industrial Technology,
Mechanical Engineering, Nursing, Health-Care Administration, Criminal
Justice, Medical Technology, Dental Hygiene, Public Administration,
Computer Science, Accounting, Mathematics, Chemistry, Agriculture and
Home Economics.

Financial:

Costs fall into four areas--maintenance, tuition, room and board and
special fees. As an in-state, undergraduate student living on campus you
could expect to pay $853 per semester with an additional $1,420 for
room and board. The average estimated cost for an out-of-state,
boarding, undergraduate is $2,744 per semester with the same cost for
room and board.

Texas College
Tyler, Texas 75712
(903) 593-8311

History:

On January 9, 1894, Texas College was organized, nestled among trees on a hill, as a Liberal Arts college. Reverend O.T. Womack served as the first president and was ably supported by Bishop Eliaz Cottrell. In 1909, the name of Texas College was changed to Phillips University, in honor of Bishop Henry Phillips. However, the institutional name, Texas College was resumed in 1912. Texas College was granted an "A" rating in 1948 by the Southern Association of Colleges and Schools. The Institution received its first time formal academic accreditation by the Regional Body during the winter of 1970. It was reaffirmed in 1974 and 1984.

Location and Enrollment:

Texas College, a church-related institution under the supervision, care and ownership of the Christian Methodist Episcopal Church, is located in Tyler, Texas, which is 100 miles east of Dallas and 90 miles west of Shreveport, Louisiana. Tyler has a population of 80,000 and is the major city of East Texas. It is so strategically located that it is within a 200-mile radius of one half of the black population of Texas. The student body has 90 percent minority backgrounds. The current enrollment is approximately 425 students.

Curriculum:

Texas College offers both Bachelor of Arts and Bachelor of Science Degrees. Courses required for career options in Pre-Law, Pre-Medicine and programs offered represent gateways to various occupational choices. Course work may be pursued in non-degree subject matter fields including: Drama, Economics, French, Geography, Physics, Spanish and Speech.

Financial:

No student is denied admission to Texas College for reasons of lack of money or racial origin. Types of assistance include: Presidential Scholars Program, Academic Scholarships and Performance Scholarships. Tuition, fees, room and board are estimated at $8,531 per academic year.

Texas Southern University
Houston, Texas 77004
(713) 527-7011

History:

Texas Southern University's history dates back to 1926, when the city of Houston's Board of Education opened Houston Junior Colored College, which later became Houston College for Negroes. In March of 1947, as a result of the act of the 50th Texas Legislature, the Institution became a state university who's name was changed to Texas State University for Negroes. The name was changed to Texas Southern University in 1951.

Location and Enrollment:

The student population at the University is over 10,000+. The University is located in Houston, Texas, a city of many cultures. The college is nearby Interstates 45N, 45S and Interstate 228. Texas Southern University is only a 1 hour drive from the ocean at Galveston or a 11/2 hour drive from the ocean at Freeport Beach.

Curriculum:

Texas Southern University offers programs of study leading to the following Bachelors Degrees: Accounting, Administration of Justice, Airway Science, Art, Bilingual Education, Biology, Business, Business Education, Communicative Disorders, Dietetics (Home Economics), Early Childhood Education (Elementary Education), Early Childhood Education (Home Economics), Economics, Elementary Education, English, Environmental Health, Health Administration, French, Health Education, History, Home Economics, Housing Management, Industrial Education, Industrial Technology, Information and Computing Science, Journalism, Mathematics, Medical Records, Medical Technologies, Music, Office Administration, Pharmacy, Physical Education, Physical Therapy, Physics, Political Science, Psychology, Public Affairs, Public Services, Respiratory Therapy, Secondary Education, Social Work, Sociology, Spanish, Spanish Education, Speech Communication, Telecommunications, Theater/Cinema, Transportation.

Financial:

Approximate cost per semester for tuition and fees is $650, room and board is $1,660. Out-of-state tuition per semester is $2,677. Seventy-five percent of the students at Texas Southern University require some form of financial aid and the Institution participates in loan programs, grants, scholarships and employment.

Tougaloo College
Tougaloo, Mississippi 39147
(601) 977-7700

History:

Tougaloo College was founded in 1869 when the American Missionary
Association purchased the plantation on which it is located. The
campus setting is that of a family oriented atmosphere. The beauty and
elegance of the tall live oaks and hanging moss, shadow the unique
architecture of such buildings as Woodworth Chapel, the centerpiece of
the campus.

Location and Enrollment:

Tougaloo College is a small, fully accredited, liberal arts institution
nestled on 500 acres in Tougaloo, Mississippi. Tougaloo College gives its
1,000 students a sense of purpose, respect and responsibility, striving
towards excellence.

Curriculum:

The College is noted for producing Teachers, Lawyers, Researchers,
Chemists and Physicists. There is an excellent Pre-Medical and Pre-
Dental track record which has produced 40 percent of all health and legal
professionals in the state of Mississippi. The curriculum is based on
semester hours. To graduate, a student must earn a C(2.0) average. The
124 semester hours are subdivided into approximately 60 semester
hours in General Education, 27 to 48 semester hours are taken in one
major department, and the remainder in electives. The College offers 3
degrees: the Bachelor of Arts, Science and Associate Arts.
Undergraduate majors offered under the *Division of Education* include
Early Childhood and Elementary Education, Arts, English, Music, Biology,
Physics, Accounting, Computer Science and Business Administration.

Financial:

Tuition, fees, room and board for Tougaloo are estimated at $7,480 a
year. Cost for students who commute is $5,020.

Tuskegee University
Tuskegee, Alabama 36088
(205) 727-8500

History:

The multi-dimensions of the work done at Tuskegee Institute promote an
historic idea of a university --a center of learning and service founded by
men who had "a love for mankind". Tuskegee was founded in 1881 and is
now a private, four-year college.

Location and Enrollment:

The 5,189-acre campus of Tuskegee Institute is located in Tuskegee,
Alabama in a rural setting. The city of Montgomery, Alabama is 40 miles
away. The campus facilities are conveniently located in 161 buildings.
The approximate full-time enrollment at the College totals nearly 4,000
students.

Curriculum:

Tuskegee is noted for its exceptional undergraduate animal science
program and the School of Veterinary Medicine. Eighty-five percent of the
nation's black veterinarians were trained at Tuskegee. Degrees offered
include: Baccalaureate-Social Sciences, Natural Sciences, Agriculture,
Education, Engineering, Home Economics and Food Administration,
Architecture and Industrial Technology, Nursing, Physical Education,
Accounting, Business Administration. Graduate degrees include
Chemistry, Biology, Agriculture, Engineering, Home Economics and Food
Administration, Education, Adult Education, Public Health Nutrition,
Veterinary Medicine and Environmental Sciences. Tuskegee also offers a
major in Forestry, another non-traditional area for African-Americans. The
Society of American Foresters reports that a significant number of
African-American professional foresters in the U.S., began their training
at Tuskegee's Forest Resource Program. Army ROTC and Aerospace
studies are also offered.

Financial:

Semester cost at Tuskegee for tuition and fees is approximately $3,367
and $1,697 for room and board. Eighty-five percent of the students
receive financial aid. Tuskegee participates in loan, grant and
employment programs.

Virgin Islands, University of the
St. Thomas, U.S Virgin Island 00802
(809) 776-9200 or Kingshill, St. Croix,
U.S. Virgin Island 00851 (809) 778-1620

History:

March 16, 1962, the College of the Virgin Islands was established. In the spring of the same year, an interim administrator was appointed to prepare the groundwork for the opening of the College in 1963. The Institution's name was changed to the University of the Virgin Islands in 1986 to better reflect the growth and diversification of its academic programs, community and regional service and research.

Location and Enrollment:

The University is spread over two campuses, with a total enrollment of 3,500 students. The St. Thomas campus is three miles west of the town of Charlotte Amalie, overlooking Brewer's Bay. The St. Croix campus is located at Golden Grove, midway between the towns of Christiansted and Frederiksted.

Curriculum:

Majors in Bachelors of Arts programs are as follows: Accounting, Biology, Business Administration, Caribbean Studies, Chemistry, Elementary Education, English, Humanities, Marine Biology, Mathematics, Music Education, Psychology, Spanish, Social Sciences, Vocational Education and Social Work. In the field of Secondary Teacher Education, courses are offered leading to certification. Majors in bachelor of science programs in the following areas: Biology, Chemistry with Physics, Marine Biology and Nursing. A Cooperative Engineering Program, whereby students complete initial studies, then transfer to an Institution for specialized study and/or training. Associate in Arts Degree programs in Accounting, Banking and Finance, Business Management, Office Assistance and Administration, Physics and Police Science and Administration. Evening and extension programs are scheduled.

Financial:

Residents pay $798 per semester and cost for non-residents is $2,298, room and board is $2,150. American citizens, permanent residents of the United States and non-resident students who graduated from local secondary schools are eligible to apply for financial assistance. Other foreign students may only apply for special foreign scholarships.

Virginia Seminary and College
Lynchburg, Virginia 24501
(804) 528-5276

History:

Virginia Seminary and College was founded in 1888 at its present location. The College is a private institution of higher learning with roots which go back as far as the need of Black students to receive an advanced education without regards to financial background. The seminary doors have always been open to whomever wished to attend.

Location and Enrollment:

The main campus contains less than 10 acres with the seminary owning two farms (more than 50 acres combined), and a rock quarry which produces an income for the institution. The current enrollment at the college totals 300 full-time students.

Curriculum:

Bachelor Degrees are offered in Theology and Christian Education. Graduate Degrees are offered, as well as Master of Divinity and Master of Christian Education.

Financial:

Cost for in-state students is $150 per course; out of state is $180 per course. Room and board is $1,300. The College accepts and participates in all financial aid programs which are state and/or federally funded. Scholarships are accepted, as well as given to students which demonstrate criteria has been met as outlined in scholarship requirements. Virginia Seminary and College searches for means for every interested student to obtain an education.

Virginia State University
Petersburg, Virginia 23803
(804) 524-5000

History:

Virginia State University is an institution of higher learning, governed under authority of the Board of Visitors. The University was founded in 1882 and today is a public, four-year, coeducational institution which is accredited by Southern Association of Colleges an Schools. The University is also a land-grant facility with objectives to aid students in attaining the maximum growth in personality and achievement.

Location and Enrollment:

The 236-acre University campus is located in rural Petersburg, Virginia. The urban area of Richmond, Virginia is just 25 miles from the University. The historic campus of Virginia State includes 54 buildings with modern, state-of-the-art laboratories and facilities. The population of the University, is approximately 4,000. The faculty members total 191 (full-time) with a faculty-student ratio of 1-to-20.

Curriculum:

Virginia State University offers Baccalaureate degrees in over 30 fields of study, and Graduate degrees in 20 areas. Programs include Agriculture, Earth Science, Physics, Biology, Medical Records Technology, Economics, Guidance and Education, Business and Industrial Administration.

Financial:

In-state tuition per year totals $7,754; out-of-state tuition per year totals $11,428: room and board is included in this cost. Virginia State accepts and participates in approved financial aid programs. Eighty-five percent of the student population depends on loans, grants, scholarships and/or employment to fund their education.

Virginia Union University
Richmond, Virginia 23220
(804) 257-5600

History:

Virginia Union University has been known for 117 years as a fountain head for higher education. In 1865, there were no educational programs for black men and women and Virginia Union is dedicated to high quality education for men and women, offering equal opportunities to all races and economic groups. The University was established under the Baptist Church.

Location and Enrollment:

The 55-acre campus is located in the urban district of Richmond, the capital district of Virginia. The campus has 20 buildings which make up the University. The current enrollment in approximately 1,400 students with 67 full-time faculty members. The faculty-student ratio is 1-15.

Curriculum:

Two Degrees are offered at Virginia Union -- a Baccalaureate in over 22 subjects, and a Graduate degree in Master of Divinity. The academic calendar at Virginia Union is based on the semester system.

Financial:

Combined tuition with room and board per year is estimated at $8,900. Approximately 90 percent of the student index receives financial assistance, Virginia Union participates in: loans, grants, employment, academic scholarships and athletic scholarships.

Voorhees College
Denmark, South Carolina 29042
(803) 793-3351

History:

Most memorable about Voorhees history is the story of its founder, Elizabeth Evelyn Wright. She was a black woman in her early twenties who, in spite betrayals, arson, jealousy, threats of violence, and weariness from wandering, persevered and founded a school in Denmark, South Carolina on April 14, 1897. Voorhees became a senior degree-granting institution in 1967, and shortly thereafter received full accreditation as a liberal arts college from the Southern Association. The first class graduated from the senior college in 1968. By 1969, the College had become a member of the Association of Episcopal Colleges and the United Negro College Fund.

Location and Enrollment:

Denmark is centrally located in the state of South Carolina, County of Bamberg. The campus is divided into two sections by State Highway 12. An elongated portion of these two sections constitutes an academic core of the campus with the academic facilities located mainly south of the State Highway and the residential and related facilities located to the north. Student enrollment averages between 500 and 1,000.

Curriculum:

For the convenience of administrative work, there are four academic divisions in which Bachelor Degrees are offered: Division of Business and Economics, Division of Education/Humanities, Division of Natural Sciences, Mathematics, and Computer Science and Division of Social Sciences. The academic calendar is based on the semester system.

Financial:

Voorhees College wants no qualified student to be denied attendance because of financial need. Students wishing to apply for financial aid may secure an application form from the Financial Aid Office or their high school counselor's office. Reviews are made of each application for aid, giving consideration to the total amount of aid available for the entire student body. Combined tuition, room and board is $6,772 a year.

West Virginia State College
Institute, West Virginia 25112
(304)766-3000

History:

Founded in 1891 as an institution for blacks, West Virginia State College(WVSC) now has a student enrollment of 86 percent white, 12 percent black and 2 percent Asian and/or other origins.

Location and Enrollment:

The 85-acre campus with 29 buildings is located in the Appalachian Foothills along the Kanawha River in the suburban community of Institute. The campus is eight miles west of Charleston, the state capital. Located just 20 minutes away from Charleston Yeager Airport, it is easily accessed by commuter buses. With an enrollment of 4,500, the college is the primary institution of higher education in the metropolitan area.

Curriculum:

There are several four-year degrees offered at WVSC including Bachelor of Arts, Bachelor of Science, Regents Bachelor of Arts and an Associate in Arts. The College also offers pre-professional courses for Dentistry, Engineering, Law, Nursing, Optometry, Pharmacy and Veterinary Science. A post-graduate certificate is offered in Accounting. Tutoring and other assistance is also available.

Financial:

Prospective students desiring financial aid should request an application form from the College. Applicants are required to file a Financial Aid Form which may be used for Pell Grants and WV Higher Education Grant Programs. Other Programs available are Supplemental Educational Opportunity Grant, National Direct Student Loan, Guaranteed Student Loan, College Work Study and scholarships based on academic performance or talent in a specific category. Combined tuition, fees, room and board for residents per semester is $2,522. Non-residents pay $3,722 per semester.

Wilberforce University
Wilberforce, Ohio 45384
(513) 376-2911
1-800-367-8565 (in Ohio)
1-800-367-8568 (outside Ohio)

History:

Founded in the State of Ohio in 1856, with roots dating back to 1843, Wilberforce is the oldest, private, historically black liberal arts college in America, and was named after the great 18th century abolitionist, William Wilberforce. Affiliated with the African Methodist Episcopal Church, the mission of the University is derived from the founding charter, to educate students of all colors, creeds, and religious faiths, who have strong Christian ideals.

Location and Enrollment:

Wilberforce is in picturesque, rural Southern Ohio, yet close to the urban centers in Dayton, Springfield, Columbus and Cincinnati, all of which offer supplemental facilities, cultural advantages and employment opportunities. The "new" Wilberforce has been designed for a student body of 1,500, giving central attention to the liberal arts and with continuing emphasis on moral and spiritual values at the core of campus living.

Curriculum:

The University grants the following earned degrees: Bachelor of Arts and Bachelor of Science. All students must satisfactorily complete at least two Cooperative Education assignments and satisfy all co-op requirements in order to earn a degree. Students in the Dual Degree Engineering and Computer Science Programs are required to complete four (4) co-op assignments. International students are required to complete one co-op assignment. Transfer students co-op requirements depend upon the number of credit hours accepted by Wilberforce University. There are 21 academic majors available. Personal and academic counseling and tutorial services are strong features within the academic framework of the University. Student faculty ratio is 12-to-1.

Financial:

Total cost for the year is approximately $10,168 for a student living on campus.

Wiley College
Marshall, Texas 75670
(903) 938-8341

History:

Wiley College was founded in 1873 and chartered in 1882, by the Freedmen's Aid Society, which later became the Board of Education for Negroes, now merged with the Board of Education of the United Methodist Church. The College is a Christian co-educational institution named for Bishop Isaac W. Wiley. It was originally located in two frame buildings, just south of Marshall city limits. In 1880, Wiley was moved to its present site, consisting of 63 acres of wooded land. Under the prudent guidance of Dr. J.S.Scott, who became the 9th president in 1948, the college continued to move forward in its physical plant and its intellectual and spiritual program.

Location and Enrollment:

Wiley College is an historically black, four-year, Methodist co-educational institution with a close personal Christian environment, promoting excellence. Students function effectively in a pluralistic society. The current enrollment is 600.

Curriculum:

Degrees are offered in a liberal arts and teaching program. Area of Humanities includes English, French, Spanish, Religion and Philosophy, Music and Art. Academic credit will be awarded for successful completion of Cooperative Education Programs. The educational aims and objectives of the institution are to provide specialized training in designated occupations, pre-professional and professional areas including: a) Teachers for Elementary and Secondary Schools; b) Pre-professional training and skills for the fields of Medicine, Dentistry, Pharmacy, Engineering, Law, Social Work, Music, Ministry; c) Business and Industry. The various academic programs include Area of Natural Sciences and Mathematics, Area of Business and Social Science, Area of Education and Teacher Training, and Basic Studies.

Financial:

Tuition, general fees, room and board will cost a student living on campus approximately $6,618/yr. For an off-campus student, the tuition and general fees will cost approximately $3,846/yr. There are laboratory fees included in the above cost, also special fees. Special awards given to students with the highest grade average. Also, scholarships are available to students.

Winston-Salem State University
Winston-Salem, North Carolina 27110
(919) 750-2070

History:

Since 1892, when Winston-Salem State University was founded as Slater Industrial Academy, academic excellence has been a tradition. Today, WSSU is proud of its outstanding faculty. Most members have earned Doctoral Degrees and are actively involved in professional and academic organizations.

Location and Enrollment:

Winston-Salem State University is a four-year, coeducational institution located in northwestern North Carolina. WSSU is located near downtown Winston-Salem in what is known as North Carolina's Triad area. It's just a short drive from WSSU to the other two cities in the Triad, Greensboro and High Point. Personalized instruction is the norm at WSSU where the student/faculty ratio is an attractive 15-1. On the average, 2,500 students and 140 faculty interact in a friendly, supportive learning environment.

Curriculum:

Degree programs are offered in nine departments: Business and Economics; Education and Physical Education; English and Foreign Languages; Fine Arts; Life Sciences; Mathematics/Computer Science; Nursing and Allied Health; Physical Sciences and Social Sciences. The University offers major programs leading to the Bachelor of Arts, Bachelor of Science and Bachelor of Science in Applied Science Degrees. Students may earn a second Bachelor's Degree by meeting requirements for both degrees. From Business Administration to Nursing, Computer Science to Mass Communications, WSSU prepares students to become professional at the top of their fields.

Financial:

Students wishing to be considered for financial assistance should apply for admission to the University as early as possible. The deadline for applications for financial aid is open, and all awards are made on a first-come, first-serve basis. Combined tuition, fees, room and board are estimated at $4,142 per year for residents. Non-residents pay approximately $9,506.

Xavier University
New Orleans, Louisiana 70125
(504) 483-7388

History:

Xavier University of Louisiana can trace its roots back to 1915, when the secondary school from which it evolved was founded by the Venerable Mother Katharine Drexel and the Sisters of the Blessed Sacrament, a religious community she established to serve American Indians and Blacks. Xavier became a reality in 1925 with the establishment of the College of Liberal Arts and Sciences. A College of Pharmacy was added in 1927. The University moved to its present campus in 1933.

Location and Enrollment:

Xavier, the only predominantly black Catholic University in the United States, is a small urban university, located near the heart of New Orleans. Enrollment at Xavier is increasing more and more each year. The current enrollment at Xavier is approximately 3,000. By race, the student body is 90 percent black and 10 percent non-black. Nearly 50 percent are non-Catholic.

Curriculum:

Xavier offers training in some three dozen academic and professional fields. The educational program is liberal arts oriented, with all students required to take a core of prescribed courses in Theology and Philosophy, the Arts and the Humanities, Communications, History and the Behavioral Sciences, and Mathematics and the Natural Sciences. Despite its liberal arts orientation, however, Xavier has received national recognition for its strong Natural Science, Pre-Health and Pharmacy programs.

Financial:

Combined tuition, fees, room and board is approximately $10,300 per year. Financial aid is available to all students based on need, and scholarships are awarded for demonstrated academic ability and special talents. 85 percent of all Xavier students receive some form of financial assistance.

A GUIDE TO FINANCIAL AID AND SCHOLARSHIPS

The first place to begin your quest for financial assistance is right in your own community. Local organizations, clubs, labor unions and private institutions are great resources for scholarships. Many large corporations have special funds set aside for education. You need to learn about as many sources for aid as you can. The following is a partial list of scholarship sources:

21st Century Scholarship Program
Annenberg General Foundation United Negro College Fund
500 East 62nd Street
New York, NY 10021
Check school's financial aid program
Discipline: General

4-H College Scholarship
National 4-H Council
7100 Connecticut Avenue
Chevy Chase, MD 20815
$1,000
Discipline: General · Deadline: October 1

ABWA
American Business Womens Association
9100 Ward Parkway
P.O. Box 8728
Kansas City, MO 64114
Discipline: Business

Academy of Television Arts and Sciences
4605 Lankership Boulevard
Hollywood, CA 91602
Limited number of $1,000 scholarships and an intern program
Discipline: Television · Deadline: February

ADHA-Warner Lambert Scholarships
ADHA Foundation Scholarship Program
444 North Michigan #3400
Chicago, IL 60611
$1,000 scholarships (5)
Discipline: Dental Hygiene · Deadline: May

Agnes Jones Jackson Scholarship
NAACP National Office Education Department
4805 Mt. Hope Drive
Baltimore, MD 21215
Undergraduates $1,500, Graduates $2,500; renewable
Discipline: General · Deadline: January 1 & April 15

AIA Minority Disadvantaged Scholarship Program
American Institute of Architects Foundation (AIAF)
1735 New York Avenue NW
Washington, DC 20006
Twenty scholarships per academic year; renewable for two years
Discipline: Architecture · Deadline: December 1 & January 1

AIAA Scholarship
American Institute Aeronautics & Astro.
1633 Broadway
New York, NY 10019
Four years, $1,000 per year
Discipline: General · Deadline: January

Air Force ROTC Scholarships
AFROTC/RROO
Maxwell AFB, AL 36112-6666
Full tuition plus $100 monthly allowance
Discipline: Scientific/Technical · Deadline: December

Alabama State University Presidential Scholarship
915 South Jackson Street
Montgomery, AL 36195-0301
$3,000-$4,000
Discipline: General

Alliance of Independent Colleges of Art Scholarships
633 East Street NW
Washington, DC 20004
Over $40,000 offered by eight leading art colleges
Discipline: Visual Arts · Deadline: February

Alpha Kappa Alpha Scholarships
5656 South Stony Island Avenue
Chicago, IL 60637
Award varies each year
Discipline: General

**American Dental Hygienist Association
Foundation Scholarship Program**
ADHA Foundation Scholarship Program
444 North Michigan #3400
Chicago, IL 60611
Awards to $1,500
Discipline: Dental Hygiene · Deadline: May

American Fund for Dental Health Fellowship
211 East Chicago Avenue
Chicago, IL 60611
$2,000
Discipline: Dentistry · Deadline: May 1

American Geological Institute
4220 King Street
Alexandria, VA 22302
$10,000 for undergraduate students and up to $4,000 for graduates
Discipline: Geosciences · Deadline: February 1

American Geological Institute Scholarships
4222 King Street
Alexandria, Va 22302
About 46 awards, $500 to $1,500
Discipline: Geoscience · Deadline: February

American Institute of Architecture
1735 New York Avenue
Washington, DC 20006
Up to $1,500. Renewable up to two years
Discipline: Architecture · Deadline: December 1

American Institute of Certified Public Accountants
AICPA
1211 Avenue of the Americas
New York, NY 10036
Approximately 400; renewable scholarships up to $1,500 per year
Discipline: Accounting · Deadline: July

American Nurses Association Minority Fellowship
1030 15th Street, N.W. Ste. 716
Washington, DC 20005
$9,000 (3 programs each has a different financial range)
Discipline: Nursing · Deadline: January 15

American Society of Newspaper Editors Foundation Scholarship
Minority Affairs Director
P.O. Box 17004
Washington, DC 20041
$750 scholarships awarded to 40 high school seniors annually
Discipline: Journalism · Deadline: November

AMOCO Scholarships
AMOCO Foundation
200 East Randolph Drive
Chicago, IL 60601
$700; renewable scholarships at 10 schools
Discipline: Geology/geophyc

American Dental Hygienists' Assoc Institute for Oral Health
444 North Michigan Avenue Ste. 3400
Chicago, IL 60611
Up to $1,500 maximum; unspecified number of scholarships
Discipline: Dentistry · Deadline: May 1

American Mensa Education and Research Foundation Program
Scholarship Committee
1701 West Third Street
Brooklyn, NY 11223
Over 30 awards $2000 to $1,000
Discipline: General · Deadline: March

AMVETS Scholarships
Western Hills Post #41
P. O. Box 11050
Cincinnati, OH 45211
Four and two year scholarships
Discipline: General · Deadline: April

Gladys C. Anderson
American Foundation for the Blind Scholarship
15 W. 16th Street
New York, NY 10011
Two awards, up to $1,000 for legally blind women
Discipline: Religion or Classical Music • Deadline: April 1

American Association of University Women
2401 Virginia Avenue, N.W.
Washington, DC 20036
Discipline: Law

ARMA Scholarship Fund
P.O. Box 8540
Prairie Village, KS 66208
About $600
Discipline: Records Management · Deadline: April

Army ROTC Scholarships
P.O. Box 9000
Clifton, NJ 07015-9974
Full tuition plus $1,000 stipend
Discipline: General · Deadline: August or December

Art Recognition and Talent Search
ARTS
P.O. Box 2876
Princeton, NJ 08541
Scholarships of $500 to $4,000
Discipline: Dance, Music, etc · Deadline: October

Arts Recognition and Talent Search
ARTS Office
300 NE 2nd Avenue
Miami, FL 33132
$400,000 in cash awards
Discipline: Music, Dance, etc · Deadline: May

Associated Male Choruses of America Scholarship Fund
P.O. Box 771
Brainerd, MN 56401
Five $475 (maximum) scholarships per year; renewable
Discipline: Music · Deadline: February 8

AT&T Dual Degree Scholarship Program
AT&T Bell Laboratories
Crawfords Corner Road, Rm 1B-207
Holmdel, NJ 07733
Full tuition and fees
Discipline: Math, Physics, etc · Deadline: December

AT&T Engineering Scholarship Program
AT&T Bell Laboratories
Crawfords Corner Road, Rm 1B-214
Holmdel, NJ 07733
15 awards, full tuition and fees
Discipline: Engineering, etc · Deadline: February

Aviation Scholarship
Organization of Black Airline Pilots, Inc.
20 North Van Brunt Street, Ste. 200
Englewood, NJ 07631
Award: Amount varies
Discipline: Engineering, etc

Avon Scholarship Award
Avon Products Foundation Inc.
9 West 57th Street
New York, NY 10019
Eight awards, four years tuition and fees
Discipline: General

Ayn Rand Essay Contest
Ayn Rand Institute
13101 Washington Boulevard Ste.248
Los Angeles, CA 90066
1st prize $5,000, five 2nd $1,000, ten 3rd $500
Discipline: General · Deadline: March

Best Products Foundation Scholarship Program
CSFA Box 112A
Londonderry Turnpike, RFD 7
Manchester, NH 03104
Renewable scholarships of $300 to $1,000
Discipline: General · Deadline: March

Black American Cinema Society Awards
Western States Black Research Center
3617 Montclair Street
Los Angeles, CA 90018
Three grants per year: 1 $750 grant, 1 $1000 grant, 1 $1500 grant
Discipline: General · Deadline: March 10

Breakthrough to Nursing Scholarship
National Student Nurses' Association
555 West 57th Street
New York, NY 10019
$1,500 stipend; five awarded each year
Discipline: Nursing · Deadline: January

Business and Professional Womens Foundation
2012 Massachusetts Avenue, N.W.
Washington, DC 20036
Discipline: Business

Cal Grant A or B California Student Aid Commission
P.O. Box 942845
Sacramento, CA 94245
Amount varies; renewable up to three years; $300 to $5,250
Discipline: General · Deadline: March

Cape Foundation, Inc.
550 Pharr Road, NE, Suite 605
Atlanta, GA 30305
Two grants totaling $4,510
Discipline: Atlanta Institute

Carl D. Perkins Scholarship Program
State Student Incentive Grant Section, US Dept of Ed
400 Maryland Avenue S.W.
Washington, DC 20002
Up to $5,000 each year
Discipline: Education

Catholic Negro Scholarship
73 Chestnut Street
Springfield, MA 01103
Varies; most awards are $300; renewable
Discipline: General · Deadline: January

Century III Leaders Program
National Assn. of Secondary School Principals
1904 Association Drive
Reston, VA 22091
About 15 awards $500 to $10,000
Discipline: Leadership · Deadline: October

Challenger Astronauts Memorial Scholarship Program
Florida Department of Education
Knott Building
Tallahassee, FL 32399
Seven $1000 scholarships per academic year; renewable up to 4 years
Discipline: Education/Arts · Deadline: March

Chemical Engineering Scholarship
Jeffrey R. Leist, Westinghouse materials Co.
P.O. Box 398704
Cincinnati, OH 45239
Award: $600
Discipline: Chemical Engineer · Deadline: March

Cincinnati Milacron Foundation Scholarships
Scholarship Committee
4701 Marburg Avenue
Cincinnati, OH 45209
Discipline: Engineering · Deadline: February

Club Managers Association of America
P.O. Box 34482
7615 Winterberry Place
Washington, DC 20034
Several $1,000; renewable scholarships
Discipline: Hotel Management · Deadline: July

Coca-Cola USA Share The Dream Scholarship Sweepstakes
P.O. Box 52107
Knoxville, TN 37950
Two $25,000 awards; eight $10,000 awards
Discipline: General · Deadline: March 29

College of Insurance Cooperative Education Program
College of Insurance (New York City)
123 William Street
New York, NY 10038
Three hundred $900 scholarships per semester; renewable
Discipline: Business & Economics · Deadline: February

Cowling Scholarships for Third World Students
Carleton College
Office of Admissions
Northfield, MN 55057
Ten four year scholarships
Discipline: General

Cox Newspaper Minority Scholarship Program
P.O.Box 4689
Atlanta, GA 30302
Expenses cover entire college fees and tuition. internship 4 years
Discipline: Journalism · Deadline: April

Crown Scholarships
Illinois Institute of Technology
10 West 33rd Street
Chicago, IL 60616
Five year scholarship, full tuition
Discipline: Architecture · Deadline: February

Delta Sigma Scholarship Award
Scholarship Committee, Delta Sigma Theta Sorority
3609 Congress Avenue
Cincinnati, OH 45213
Limited number of awards $750 each
Discipline: General

Dietrich/Cross Scholarship
Assoc of Former Agents of the US Secret Service
P.O.Box 11681
Alexandria, VA 22312
One or more $1,000 scholarship per year;non-renewable
Discipline: Law Enforcement

Digital Equipment Corporation
2500 West Union Hills Drive
Phoenix, AZ 85027
$1,000
Discipline: General · Deadline: August

Distributive Education Clubs of America (DECA-Schlrshps)
1908 Association Drive
Reston, VA 22091
Award varies
Discipline: General · Deadline: March

Duracell/National Urban League Scholarship
National Urban League
500 East 62nd Street
New York, NY 10021
Five awards up to $10,000
Discipline: Varies •   Deadline: April

Earl Warren Legal Training Program Scholarships
99 Hudson Street, 16th Floor
New York, NY 10013
Award varies
Discipline: Law · Deadline: March

Eastman Kodak Company
343 State Street
Rochester, NY 14650
Award covers 100% of tuition; renewed annually
Discipline: Engineering, etc

Edison/McGraw Scholarship Program

National Science Teachers Association
P.O.Box 2800
La Jolla, Ca 92038
Two $5,000 scholarships; ten $1,000 scholarships
Discipline: Science/Engineering · Deadline: December 1

Educational Communications Scholarship Foundation

721 North McKinley Road
Lake Forest, IL 60045
At least 50 awards of $1,000 each
Discipline: General · Deadline: June

Educational Fund Grant

Johnson Products
8522 South Lafayette
Chicago, IL 60620
Award varies
Discipline: General · Deadline: August

Engineering Foundation of Ohio

Peter Marshall, P.E.
2250 Bretton Drive
Cincinnati, OH 45244
Award varies
Discipline: Engineering · Deadline: November

Engineering Incentive Grants Program

National Action Council for Minorities
3 West 35th Street
New York, NY 10001
Number of awards varies, $2,500 maximum
Discipline: Engineering

Engineering Scholarship Program General Electric Foundation

The College Board
45 Columbus Avenue
New York, NY 10023
Up to $4,000
Discipline: Business, Engineering · Deadline: November 15

Esper A. Peterson Foundation

1300 Skokie Highway
Gurnee, IL 60031
Grants totaling $21,200
Discipline: General; IL residents · Deadline: January 1

Estelle Massey Osborne Scholarship

Nurses Educational Fund
555 West 57th Street
New York, NY 10019
$2,500-$10,000; non-renewable
Discipline: Nursing · Deadline: August 1

Ethnic Minority Pharmacy Scholarships

National Pharmaceutical Foundation Inc.
P.O.Box 5439
Takoma Park, MD 20910
Twelve $500-$1,000(maximum) scholarships per year; renewable
Discipline: Pharmacy

Ethnic Minority Pharmacy Scholarships

National Pharmaceutical Foundation, Inc.
1728 17th Street N.E.
Washington, DC 20002
Award varies
Discipline: General

Fitzgibbon Scholarship Competition

Washington University
P.O.Box 1089
St. Louis, MO 63130
Full tuition plus $1,000 stipend
Discipline: General

Foundation for Exceptional Children Scholarship Awards

1920 Association Drive
Reston, VA 22091
$1,000 for disabled minority or disabled gifted minority
Discipline: General • Deadline: January 1

Foundation of the National Student Nurses Association Scholarship Program

555 West Street Ste. 1325
New York, NY 10019
$1,000-$2,500
Discipline: Nursing · Deadline: February 1

Gardner Foundation Scholarship Award

The Gardner Foundation
407 Charles Street
Middletown, OH 45042
16 awards, $1,100
Discipline: General · Deadline: April

Herbert Lehman Education Fund Scholarships
99 Hudson Street #1600
New York, NY 10013
$1,000
Discipline: General · Deadline: April 15

Honda Scholarship Program
Any of 35 OFIC member colleges
$1,000
Discipline: General

Howard Brown Rickard Scholarship
National Federation of the Blind
814 Fourth Ave #200
Grinnell, IA 50112
Award: $2,500
Discipline: Varies • Deadline: March

"I Have A Dream" Foundation Scholarships
31 West 34th Street
New York, NY 10001
Award: Varies
Discipline: General

Incentive Grants Program
National Action Council for Minorities in Engineering
3 West 35th Street
New York, NY 10001
$250-$2,500
Discipline: Engineering

Institute of Food Technologists Scholarships
Scholarship Department
221 North LaSalle
Chicago, IL 60601
A number of scholarships from $500 to $6,000 per year
Discipline: Food Technology · Deadline: February

International Brotherhood of Teamsters Scholarship Fund
25 Louisiana Avenue N.W.
Washington, DC 20001
Twenty-five $1,000 Scholarships
Discipline: General · Deadline: November

Irwin Auger Scholarship
Irwin Auger Bit Company Foundation
132 Grant Street
Wilmington, OH 45177
Five awards, $500 each
Discipline: General

Jackie Robinson Foundation Scholarship Fund
80 Eighth Avenue, 20th Floor
New York, NY 10011
Up to $20,000 for four years
Discipline: General • Deadline: March 31

Japan-U.S. Senate Scholarship Program
Youth for Understanding, International Exchange
3501 Newark Street NW
Washington, DC 20016
Summer in Japan
Discipline: General · Deadline: October

JCWM Scholarships
U.S. Jaycee War Memorial Fund
P.O. Box 7 - JCWM Building
Tulsa, OK 74121
Six awards $1,000 each
Discipline: General · Deadline: March

Jean Arnot Reid Scholarships
National Association of Bank Women Scholarships
500 North Michigan Avenue Ste. 1400
Chicago, IL 60611
Six awards of $2,000 to $5,000
Discipline: Banking · Deadline: June

John B. Ervin Scholarship
Ervin Scholarship Committee, Washington University
P.O.Box 1192 - 1 Brookings Drive
Saint Louis, MO 63130
Ten full tuition scholarships plus $2,500 stipend
Discipline: General · Deadline: February

Johnny Bench Scholarship
Cincinnati Scholarship Foundation
230 East 9th Street
Cincinnati, OH 45202
Limited number of renewable awards $500-$1,500
Discipline: General

Jostens Foundation Leader Scholarships
Scholarship Program
P.O.Box 88
St. Peter, MN 56082
250 scholarships of $1,00 each
Discipline: Leadership · Deadline: November

Junior Achievement Awards Program
Junior Achievement Inc.
550 Summer Street
Stamford, CT 06901
One full tuition scholarship and several cash awards $50-$1,500
Discipline: Business, etc.

Kappa Alpha Psi Scholarship Program
Kappa Alpha Psi Fraternity, Inc.
2320 North Broad Street
Philadelphia, PA 19132
Up to $800 per year; renewable
Discipline: General

Kemper (James S.) Foundation Scholar Grant
Route 22
Long Grove, IL 60049
Fifteen $1,000-$3,500 (maximum) grants per year;renewable
Discipline: Business

Knox College Presidential Scholarship
Knox College
Galesburg, IL 61401
$3,500 (10-15)
Discipline: General · Deadline: January 15

Kraft-League of United Latin American Citizens Scholarships
League of United Latin American Citizens (LULAC)
400 First Street, NW, Suite 716
Washington, DC 20001
Ten $2,500 per year
Discipline: General · Deadline: May

Kraft-National Urban League Scholarship
National Urban League-c/o Director of Education
500 East 62nd Street
New York, NY 10021
Five $10,000 scholarships/Five $1,000 scholarships
Discipline: General · Deadline: April

Lauranne Sames Scholarship Award
National Black Nurses' Association, Inc.
P.O. Box 18358
Boston, MA 02118
Award varies; renewable
Discipline: Nursing · Deadline: May each year

Law Enforcement Assistance Award
Boy Scouts of America
1325 Walnut Hill Lane
Irving, TX 75062
One $500 (maximum) scholarship per year
Discipline: Law Enforcement · Deadline: January 1

Liederkranz Foundation Scholarship
6 East 87th Street
New York, NY 10128
Sixteen $1,000-$4,000 scholarships per year; non-renewable
Discipline: Music

Lillian E. Glover Illinois PTA Scholarship Program
Illinois Congress of Parents and Teachers
901 South Spring Street
Springfield, IL 62704
$200 to $600
Discipline: Education · Deadline: March 15

Lonzie L. Jones Jr. Natl Sickle Cell Scholarship Program
National Association for Sickle Cell Disease, Inc.
4221 Wilshire Blvd Ste. 360
Los Angeles, CA 90010-3503
Award: Up to $2,500
Discipline: General • Deadline September

Louisiana Education Scholarships
LA Governor's Spcl Commission on Educational Services
P.O.Box 91202
Scholarship/Grant Division
Baton Rouge, LA 70821-9202
250- $2,000 scholarships per year; renewable up to four years
Discipline: Education · Deadline: March 1

Louisiana Paul Douglas Teachers Scholarship
LA Governor's Spcl Commission on Educational Services
P.O.Box 91202
Scholarship/Grant Division
Baton Rouge, LA 70821-9202
37- $5,000 scholarships per year; renewable up to four years
Discipline: Education · Deadline: March 1

Lulag-National Educational Service Center Scholarship
400 First Street, NW, Suite 716
Washington, DC 20001
$200-$1,000
Discipline: All Areas

M. Elizabeth Carnegie Scholarship
Nurses Educational Funds, Inc.
555 West 57 Street
New York, NY 10019
$2,000-$5,000 per year; non-renewable; full-time study only
Discipline: Nursing · Deadline: February

.Mary Jane & Jerome A. Straka Scholarship Fund
American Association for Gifted Children
15 Gramercy Park
New York, NY 10003
Renewable scholarships of various amounts
Discipline: Math, Science, Economics · Deadline: May 31

Massachusetts General Scholarships
Massachusetts Board of Regents Scholarship Office
150 Causeway Street, Rm 600
Boston, MA 02114
Approximately 45,000 $200-$3,600 (maximum) scholarships per year; renewable
Discipline: General · Deadline: May 1

Michael Jackson Scholarship Program
United Negro College Fund
500 East 62nd Street
New York, NY 10021
Check school's financial aid program
Discipline: Performing Art, Communications

Minority Disadvantaged Scholarship
The American Institute of Architects
1735 New York Avenue N.W.
Washington, DC 20006
$500-$3,000
Discipline: Architects · Deadline: December 1

Minority Disadvantaged Scholarship Program
American Institute of Architects
135 New York Avenue, NW
Washington, DC 20006
$400 to $3,000; renewable for three years
Discipline: Architecture · Deadline: March

Minority High School Research Apprentice Program
National Inst of Health-Division of Research Resources
9000 Rockville Pike Rm #5B-23 Bldg 31
Bethesda, MD 20892
$1,500
Discipline: Medical · Deadline: December 1

Minority Reporting Intern Program
Dow Jones Newspaper Fund
P.O.Box 300
Princeton, NJ 08543-0300
$1,000
Discipline: General · Deadline: January

MSPE Minority Engineering Scholarship
Michigan Society of Professional Engineers
P.O.Box 10214
215 North Walnut
Lansing, MI 48901
$500
Discipline: Engineering · Deadline: December

Music Assistance Fund
New York Philharmonic Avery Fisher Hall
Broadway at 65th Street
New York, NY 10023
$500 to $2,500 per academic year, depending on need and talent
Discipline: Music · Deadline: March

NAACP ACT-SO Scholarships
Your local NAACP branch
$500 to $1,000
Discipline: Humanities, etc

NAACP Roy Wilkins Scholarships
NAACP Youth and College Division
186 Remsen Street
Brooklyn, NY 11201
$1,000 (10-12)
Discipline: General · Deadline: Early June

NAACP Willems Scholarship
NAACP National Office Education Department
4805 Mt. Hope Drive
Baltimore, MD 21215
Undergraduates $2,000; Graduates $3,000
Discipline: Math, Chemistry · Deadline: January 1 & April 15

NACME Incentive Grants Program
NACME
3 West 35th Street
New York, NY 10001
Award varies $250 to $2,500
Discipline: Engineering

NAPHCC Scholarship Program
National Assoc of Plumbing-Heating-Cooling Contractors
P.O.Box 6808
Falls Church, VA 22046
$2,500
Discipline: Engineering,etc · Deadline: May 1

NAPHCC Scholarship Program
National Assoc of Plumbing-Heating-Cooling Contractors
P.O.Box 6808
Falls Church, VA 22046
$2,500
Discipline: Business Administration · Deadline: May 1

National Achievement Scholarship Program for Outstanding Negro Students
One American Plaza
Evanston, IL 60201
About 650 scholarships. $250-$2,500 per year; renewable
Discipline: General · Deadline: Late October

National Secondary Education Council's Academy All-American
2570 Palumbo Drive
Lexington, KY 40509
Award varies
Discipline: General

National Achievement Scholarship Program
One Rotary Center
Evanston, IL 60201
350 Scholarships of $2,000;200 corporate-sponsored awards + more
Discipline: General · Deadline: October

National Action Council for Minorities in Engineering Incentive Grants
National Action Council for Minorities in Engineering-NACM, Inc.
3 West 35th Street
New York, NY 10001
$250-$2,500
Discipline: Engineering

National AMBUCS Scholarships for Therapists
P.O.Box 5127
High Point, NC 27262
About 175 awards, amount varies
Discipline: Therapy · Deadline: May & November

National Assoc of Black Accountants Student Scholarship Program
National Association of Black Accountants
300 1 Street, NE, Suite 107
Washington, DC 20002
Award varies
Discipline: Accounting

National Assoc of Black Journalists Scholarship Award
P.O. Box 17212
Washington, DC 20041
$2,500
Discipline: Journalism · Deadline: Fall

National Assoc of Black Women Attorneys Scholarship
National Association for Women Deans
1625 Eye Street, NW, Suite 626
Washington, DC 20006
$1,000
Discipline: Law

National Association of Black Accountants
900 Second Street N.E. Ste. 205
Washington, DC 20002
$2,500-$1,000
Discipline: Accounting · Deadline: Summer

National Association of Plumbing, Heating & Cooling Contractors
P.O.Box 6808
Falls Church, VA 22046
Award: $2,500
Discipline: Engineering/Construction

National Baptist Convention USA, Inc.
356 East Boulevard
Baton Rouge, LA 70802
$1,000
Discipline: General · Deadline: Fall

National Basketball Association Scholarship
645 Fifth Avenue 15th Floor
New York, NY 10022
$1,000
Discipline: General · Deadline: Mid-November

National Consortium for Graduate Degrees for Minorities
P.O.Box 537
Notre Dame, IN 46556
Award: Up to $5,000
Discipline: Engineering • Deadline December

National Honor Society Scholarship Awards Program
Division of Student Activities
1904 Association Drive
Reston, VA 22091
250 $1,000 scholarships
Discipline: General · Deadline: February

National Institute for Food Service Industry Scholarships
20 North Wacker Drive, Suite 2620
Chicago, IL 60606
$750-$2,600 for two years
Discipline: Food · Deadline: April 1

National Merit Scholarship Program
One American Plaza
Evanston, IL 60201-4897
About 3,500 scholarships: $250-$4,000 per year
Discipline: General · Deadline: Late October

National Negro Business & Professional Women's Club, Inc.
1806 New Hampshire Avenue, N.W.
Washington, DC 20009
Award varies
Discipline: General

National Newspaper Publishers Association Scholarships
948 National Press Building
Washington, DC 20045
Five $1,200 per year; renewable for up to 3 additional years
Discipline: Journalism

National Secondary Education Council's Academic All-American
2570 Palumbo Drive
Lexington, KY 40509
Discipline: General

National Scholarship Trust Fund
4615 Forbes Avenue
Pittsburgh, PA 15213
Up to $1,000
Discipline: Varies • Deadline: January 15

National Society of Professional Engineers Education Foundation
1420 King Street
Alexandria, VA 22314
Award: $1000-$4,000
Discipline: Engineering • Deadline November 15

National Society of Professional Engineers
2029 K Street NW
Washington, DC 20006
Over 150 $1,000-full tuition scholarships. Renewable
Discipline: Engineering · Deadline: September

National Society of Public Accountants Scholarships
1717 Pennsylvania Avenue, NW
Washington, DC 20006
Awards 22-$1,000 per year
Discipline: Accounting · Deadline: February

National Pharmaceutical Foundation, Inc
Box 5439
Takoma Park, MD 20910
Award: Twelve $500-$1,000 per academic year, renewable

National Technical Association
P.O. Box 7045
Washington, DC 20021
Awards: Varies
Discipline: Finance, Engineering • Deadline: May

National Writing Competition for H.S. Journalism Workshops
Dow Jones Newspaper Fund
P.O.Box 300
Princeton, NJ 08543-0300
$1,000 each year; renewable for up to 3 additional years
Discipline: Journalism

Navy-Marine Corps NROTC Scholarships
Navy Recruiter or Write Navy Opportunity, Info Center (05)
P.O.Box 5000
Clifton, NJ 07015-9939
Full tuition plus $100 month allowance
Discipline: General · Deadline: December

NC Prospective Teacher Scholarship Loan
North Carolina Department of Public Education
116 West Edenton Street
Raleigh, NC 27603-1712
200 $2,000 scholarships per year; renewable
Discipline: Education

Negro Educational Emergency Drive Scholarship Program
497 Union Trust Building
Pittsburgh, PA 15219
$100-$1,000
Discipline: General · Deadline: May 13

New York Telephone Minority Scholarship Program
Citizens' Scholarship Foundation of America, Inc.
P.O.Box 297 - 1505 Riverview Road
St. Peter, MN 56082
Award varies
Discipline: General

Newspaper Fund Scholarship/Internship
The Newspaper Fund
P.O.Box 300
Princeton, NJ 08540
About 60 Awards $1,000 for general, $1,500 for minorities
Discipline: Journalism · Deadline: Thanksgiving

Newtonville Woman's Club Scholarship
1398 MA State Federation of Women's Club (MSFWC)
P.O.Box 679 - 245 Dutton Road
Sudbury, MA 01776
One $600 scholarship for Education/Training
Discipline: Education · Deadline: March 15

NAHJ Scholarships
NAHJ National Press Bldg
Suite 1193
Washington, DC 20045
Thirty awards up to $1,000
Discipline: Journalism • Deadline: December 31

NIFI-Griffith Laboratories Scholarships
National Institute for the Food Service Industry
20 N. Wacker Dr. Suite 2620
Chicago, IL 60606
$3,000 for two years
Discipline: Culinary Arts · Deadline: April

NIFI-Nestle's Scholarship
National Institute for Food Service Industry
20 N. Wacker Dr. Suite 2620
Chicago, IL 60606
$1,500 for two years
Discipline: Culinary Arts · Deadline: April

NSPE Engineering Scholarship at Prairie View A&M University
National Society of Professional Engineers
1420 King Street
Alexandria, VA 22314
$1,000
Discipline: Engineering · Deadline: November 15

NSPE Engineering Scholarship at Polytechnic University
National Society of Professional Engineers
1420 King Street
Alexandria, VA 22314
$1,500
Discipline: Engineering · Deadline: November 15

NSPE Minority Scholarships
National Society of Professional Engineers Educational Foundation
1420 King Street
Alexandria, VA 22314
Three $1,000 each year
Discipline: General · Deadline: December

Ohio Academic Scholarship Program
Ohio Board of Regents
30 East Broad Street Rm 3600
Columbus, OH 43215
$1,000
Discipline: General · Deadline: February 23

Ohio Air National Guard
Headquarters Ohio Air National Guard
2825 West Granville Road
Worthington, OH 43085
Pays average state tuition plus $140 per month
Discipline: General

Ohio War Orphans Scholarships
Ohio Board of Reagents, 3600 State Office Tower
30 East Broad Street
Columbus, OH 43215
Discipline: General · Deadline: July

Omega Psi Phi Emergency Aid
Omega Psi Phi Fraternity
2714 Georgia Avenue, NW
Washington, DC 20001
Up to $300
Discipline: General

Omega Psi Phi Undergraduate & Graduate Scholarships
Omega Psi Phi Fraternity
2714 Georgia Avenue, NW
Washington, DC 20001
$500-$2,000 per year
Discipline: General · Deadline: January

Omega Psi Phi Dist & Natl "Scholar-of-the-year"Awards
Omega Psi Phi Fraternity
2714 Georgia Avenue, NW
Washington, DC 20001
11 district schlrs win a certificate and $500; natl winner $1,000
Discipline: General · Deadline: 30 days after meet

Oprah Winfrey Scholars Morehouse College
830 West View Drive S.W.
Atlanta, GA 30314
Full Scholarships
Discipline: General

Orville Redenbacher's Second Start Scholarship Program
P.O.Box 4137
Blair, NE 68009
$1,000
Discipline: General · Deadline: March 1 & May 1

Pharmaceutical Manufacturers Association Foundation
1100 15th Street, NW
Washington, DC 20005
Award: Eight $10,000 fellowships during thesis research
Discipline: Pharmacology • Deadline: February

Phi Delta Kappa Educational Foundation Scholarships
P.O.Box 789
8th Street & Union Avenue
Bloomington, IN 47401
$750 to $1,500
Discipline: Education · Deadline: February

Prairie View A&M Univ Minority Engineering Effort Scholarships
Prairie View A&M University
Drawer C
Prairie View, TX 77445
$250-$2,500
Discipline: Engineering · Deadline: August 1

Presbyterian Church-USA (Student Opportuntiy Minority Scholarships)
475 Riverside Dr Rm 430
New York, NY 10115
Between 110 and 130 $100-$1,400 per year , renewable
Discipline: General • Deadline April

President's Committee on Employment of the Handicapped
(National Journalism Contest for the Handicapped)
1111 20th Street NW 6th Floor
Washington, DC 20036
Award: $1,000-$3,000
Discipline: General • Deadline: January

Printing, Publishing and Packaging Industry School
National Scholarship Fund of Graphic Arts Industry
4615 Forbes Avenue
Pittsburgh, PA 15213
Awards can range up to $1,000
Discipline: Graphic Communications · Deadline: January

Robin Scholarship Fund
1333 North Wells Street
Chicago, IL 60610
88 grants totaling $160,454; range, $130-$3,750
Discipline: Illinois High School students · Deadline: January 15

Roy Wilkins Scholarship
NAACP Youth and College Division
4805 Mt Hope Drive
Baltimore, MD 21215
$500-$1,000
Discipline: All Areas · Deadline: January 1-May 1

Ruth Jenkins Scholarship Fund
Doris Towne, Trust Administrator
233 North Fair Oaks
Pasadena, CA 91103
Eight grants totaling $4,550; high, $1,150, low $400
Discipline: San Diego, CA · Deadline: May 31

S.E. Natl Scholarship Service & Fund for Negro Students
965 Martin Luther King Drive
Atlanta, GA 30314
Not applicable
Discipline: General Sachs Foundation

United Bank Tower
90 South Cascade Avenue Ste. 1410
Colorado Spring, CO 80903
$,1000 for undergraduates, $4,000 for graduates; renewable
Discipline: General · Deadline: January 1

Sadie T. M. Alexander Scholarship
Delta Sigma Theta Sorority
1707 New Hampshire Avenue, NW
Washington, DC 20009
Award varies
Discipline: Law · Deadline: March 1

SAE/Uniroyal Scholarship Program
400 Commonwealth Drive
Warrendale, PA 15096
$2,000
Discipline: Engineering · Deadline: December 15

SAMPE Undergraduate Scholarship Award in Engineering & Science
Society for the Advancement of Material & Process Engineering
P.O.Box 2459 - 668 South Azusa Avenue
Covina, CA 91722
27- $1,000 (maximum) awards per year; renewable
Discipline: Chemistry · Deadline: March

Santa Fe Pacific Railway Foundation Grant Program
National Center for Indian Education
P.O.Box 18239
Capitol Hill Station
Denver, CO 80218
Up to $2,000 per year for four years
Discipline: Business, etc · Deadline: March 15

Scholastic Art Awards
Scholastic Ind.
730 Broadway
New York, NY 10003
About 100 full tuition scholarships; various cash awards
Discipline: Art · Deadline: February

Scholastic Photography Award
Scholastic Inc.
730 Broadway
New York, NY 10003
About 250 in amounts of $25 to $4,000
Discipline: Photography · Deadline: February

Scholastic Writing Awards
Scholastic Inc.
730 Broadway
New York, NY 10003
Several cash awards $10 to $1,500
Discipline: Short Stories · Deadline: January

Shreve Foundation Scholarship
William & Mary Shreve Foundation, Inc.
176 Riverside Avenue
Red Bank, NJ 07701
22- awards; $1,500 maximum
Discipline: General

Society of Exploration, Geophysics Foundation Scholarship
Scholarship Committee
P.O.Box 3098
Tulsa, OK 74101
Over 80 scholarships of about $800 each
Discipline: Geophysics · Deadline: March

Society of Women Engineers Scholarships
345 East 47th Street
New York, NY 10017
Limited number of $1,000 scholarships
Discipline: Engineering · Deadline: July

Southland Scholars Program
Southland Corporation
P.O.Box 719
2828 North Haskell Avenue
Dallas, TX 75221
100 awards, four years, $1,000 per year
Discipline: General

State Farm Foundation Exceptional Student Fellowships Awards
State Farm Companies Foundation
One State Farm Plaza
Bloomington, IL 61710
30- $2,500 (maximum) fellowships per year
Discipline: Engineering · Deadline: February 28

Stillman College United Negro College Fund Scholarship
Stillman College
Tuscaloosa, AL 35403
$100-$2,000
Discipline: General

Student Opportunity Minority Scholarships
Presbyterian Church-USA
475 Riverside Drive Rm 430
New York, NY 10115
$100-$1400
Discipline: General · Deadline: April 1

Tennessee Academic Scholars Program
Tennessee Student Assistant Corporation
404 James Robertson Parkway,Ste1950
Nashville, TN 37219
14- $4,000
Discipline: General · Deadline: March 1

The Flickinger Memorial Scholarship
The Flickinger Memorial Trust, Inc.
P.O.Box 1255
115 W. North Street
Lima, OH 45802
37- awards, maximum of $2,000
Discipline: General

The James S. Williams Scholarship Foundation
P.O.Box 152
Marion, SC 29571
Full scholarships
Discipline: General · Deadline: July 15

The James W. Colgan Fund
c/o Bank of New England-West Department
P.O.Box 9003
1391 Main Street
Springfield, MA 01101
189 loans totaling $158,075; range $250-$2,000
Discipline: Resident of Mass. · Deadline: May 31

The Minority Dental Student Scholarship
American Fund for Dental Health
211 East Chicago Avenue Ste. 820
Chicago, IL 60611
$1,000
Discipline: Dentistry · Deadline: May 1

The National Black MBA Association
180 North Michigan Avenue Ste. 1820
Chicago, IL 60601
$3,000
Discipline: Management · Deadline: May 31

The National Assoc of Black Journalists Scholarship Program
P.O.Box 17212
Washington, DC 20041
$2,500
Discipline: Journalism · Deadline: March

The Starr Endowed Scholarship Fund
Bryant College
450 Douglas Pike
Smithfield, RI 02917
Tuition assistance. Amount varies
Discipline: General

Tuskegee Airmen Scholarship Fund
3933 6th Avenue
Los Angeles, CA 90008-2730
Up to $1,500
Discipline: Aviation, Aerospace • Deadline: December 1

Tuskegee University Choir Scholarship
Tuskegee University Music Department
Tuskegee, AL 36088
25 $880 awards
Discipline: General

U.S. Coast Guard Academy
Director, Candidate Guidance
United States Coast Guard Academy
New London, CT 06320
Full tuition
Discipline: General

UNCF/Toyota Scholarship Program
United Negro College Fund
500 East 62nd Street
New York, NY 10021
Check school's financial aid program
Discipline: General

Undergraduate Scholarship Awards
Educational Communications Scholarship Foundation
721 North McKinley Road
Lake Forest, IL 60045
50 awards, $1,000 each
Discipline: General

United Negro College Fund
500 East 62nd Street
New York, NY 10021
$100-$2,500 per year; renewable
Discipline: General

United Negro College Fund/Citicorp Fellowships
Citicorp
399 Park Avenue
New York, NY 10043
Award varies; renewable up to three additional years
Discipline: General

United Negro College Fund Scholarships
United States Senate Youth Program
Program Director, US Senate Youth Program
690 Market Street
San Francisco, CA 94104
Over 100 $2,000 scholarships
Discipline: Leadership · Deadline: Early Fall

University of Maryland Eastern Shore Art Scholarship
University of Maryland Eastern Shore
Princess Anne, MD 21853
$1,000
Discipline: Art, Painting · Deadline: June 30

US Merchant Marine Academy
Director, Candidate Guidance
US Merchant Marine Academy
Kings Point, NY 11024
Full tuition
Discipline: General

Voice of America Scholarship Program
Voice of Democracy Program, VFW National Headquarters
Broadway at 34th Street
Kansas City, MO 64111
Local and national awards $1,000 to $14,000
Discipline: Public Speaking · Deadline: November

Westinghouse Science Scholarships & Awards
Science Service
1719 North Street, NW
Washington, DC 20036
$1,000-$20,000

Following is a list of government-sponsored grants and loans. Be certain to find out which form is required for each school.

Pell Grants

Students must register for at least 12 credit hours and demonstrate financial hardship. There is no repayment of this grant.

Supplemental Educational Opportunity
Grant (SEOG)

Limited funds are available for students with exceptional financial needs. Undergraduates who receive Pell Grants qualify for an SEOG.

College Work - Study

Full-time students earn financial aid by working a MAXIMUM of 20 hours per week. The amount of money awarded depends on the student's needs.

Perkins Loans

A low-interest rate loan (5%) available to students who demonstrate a financial need. Students must sign a promissory note agreeing to repay. The school makes the loan and sets its own deadlines for applying.

Stafford Loans

For new borrowers, the interest rates vary depending on length of repayment -- 8% for the first 4 years, 10% thereafter. Students must sign a promissory note, agreeing to repay.

Parent Loans for Undergraduates (PLUS)

Funds are available to parents to aid financially dependent graduate or undergraduate students. Up to $4,000 a year to a maximum of $20,000 is available with variable interest rates. Loans are made in the name of the parent who must sign a promissory note, agreeing to repay.

Supplemental Loans for Students (SLS)

Qualified students who need additional funds can borrow up to $4,000 a year, to a maximum of $20,000. Students must sign a promissory note, agreeing to repay.